PORTRAIT OF
ROUTE 66

Beverly Osborne and his Chicken in the Rough Western girls going to the FFA and 4-H Club Live Stock Auction. It is the custom at Beverly's to buy a champion each year.

PORTRAIT OF

ROUTE 66

IMAGES FROM THE

CURT TEICH POSTCARD ARCHIVES

T. LINDSAY BAKER

FOREWORD BY JOE SONDERMAN

UNIVERSITY OF OKLAHOMA PRESS : NORMAN

This book is published with the generous assistance of the
Wallace C. Thompson Endowment Fund, University of Oklahoma Foundation.

Also by T. Lindsay Baker

(with Steven R. Rae, Seymour V. Connor, and Joseph E. Minor) *Water for the Southwest: Historical Survey and Guide to Historic Sites* (1973)

The Early History of Panna Maria, Texas (1975)

The First Polish Americans: Silesian Settlements in Texas (1979)

Historia najstarszych polskich osad w Ameryce [History of the Oldest Polish Settlements in America] (1981)

The Polish Texans (1982)

A Field Guide to American Windmills (1985)

Building the Lone Star: An Illustrated Guide to Historic Sites (1986)

Ghost Towns of Texas (1986)

(with Billy R. Harrison) *Adobe Walls: The History and Archeology of the 1874 Trading Post* (1986)

Lighthouses of Texas (1991)

Blades in the Sky: Windmilling Through the Eyes of B. H. "Tex" Burdick (1992)

(with Julie P. Baker) *The WPA Oklahoma Slave Narratives* (1996)

(with Julie P. Baker) *Till Freedom Cried Out: Memories of Texas Slave Life* (1997)

The Texas Red River Country: The Official Surveys of the Headwaters, 1876 (1998)

North American Windmill Manufacturers' Trade Literature: A Descriptive Guide (1999)

The 702 Model Windmill: Its Assembly, Installation and Use (1999)

More Ghost Towns of Texas (2003)

A Guide to United States Patents for Windmills and Wind Engines 1793–1950 (2004)

American Windmills: An Album of Historic Photographs (2007)

Confederate Guerrilla: The Civil War Memoir of Joseph M. Bailey (2007)

(editor) *The Birth of a Texas Ghost Town: Thurber, 1886–1933*, by Mary Jane Gentry (2008)

Gangster Tour of Texas (2011)

Texas Stories I Like to Tell My Friends: Real-Life Tales of Love, Betrayal, and Dreams from the History of the Lone Star State (2011)

More Texas Stories I Like to Tell My Friends: The Tales of Adventure and Intrigue Continue from the History of the Lone Star State (2012)

LIBRARY OF CONGRESS CATALOGING-IN-PUBLICATION DATA

Names: Baker, T. Lindsay, author.
Title: Portrait of Route 66 : images from the Curt Teich Postcard Archives / T. Lindsay Baker.
Description: Norman : University of Oklahoma Press, 2016. | Includes index.
Identifiers: LCCN 2015038369 | ISBN 978-0-8061-5341-4 (hardcover : alk. paper)
Subjects: LCSH: West (U.S.)—Pictorial works. | United States Highway 66—Pictorial works. | Historic sites—West (U.S.)—Pictorial works. | Postcards West (U.S.) | Curt Teich Postcard Archives.
Classification: LCC F590.7 .B35 2016 | DDC 978—dc23 LC record available at http://lccn.loc.gov/2015038369

The paper in this book meets the guidelines for permanence and durability of the Committee on Production Guidelines for Book Longevity of the Council on Library Resources, Inc. ∞

1 2 3 4 5 6 7 8 9 10

To my parents, Mary and Garnell Baker,

who in 1956 took me on my first road trip along Route 66

CONTENTS

CHAPTER ONE

CHAPTER THREE

CHAPTER TWO

CHAPTER FOUR

CHAPTER FIVE

TEXAS

CHAPTER SEVEN

ARIZONA

CHAPTER SIX

NEW MEXICO

CHAPTER EIGHT

CALIFORNIA

FOREWORD

JOE SONDERMAN

IT'S THE MOST FAMOUS ROAD IN THE WORLD, ingrained in our pop culture, celebrated in song, television shows, movies, and legends. In *The Grapes of Wrath* John Steinbeck called Route 66 "The Mother Road," and Nat King Cole sang "(Get Your Kicks) on Route 66." The road led refugees from the Dust Bowl to the promised land of California, a migration of workers to jobs in defense plants during World War II and families to the great vacationlands after the war. The great interstate system was necessary for safety, speed, and economic reasons. But we lost something when the travelers stopped slowing down through the business districts of our cities and towns.

Today we travel in soundproof, air-conditioned cocoons through a world sanitized for our protection. The same generic fast food joints, chain hotels, and big box retailers cluster at the interstate off-ramps. Our children, headphones blocking out the world, hardly look up from their electronic devices long enough to ask, "Are we there yet?" There is little human interaction, and as a result we are losing our sense of community. Route 66 recalls a time when travel was an adventure. It offered variety and unpredictability in the landscape, food, accommodations, and people met along the way.

The businesses were owned by families often struggling to earn a living beside the road. They didn't have corporate marketing and there was no social media. Postcards were an inexpensive way to advertise, and they played a role in establishing the road and its attractions in the minds of the public. Curt Teich was far and away the biggest producer of these cardboard calling cards during the glory years of Route 66, and the firm made sure the image presented to the public was ideal.

Now that many of the businesses along Route 66 are gone, a postcard or archive photo may provide the only remaining visual record. It is often an idealized view, as the artists for Curt Teich were adept at making the colors bright and removing unsightly obstacles such as utility poles or adding sunsets. The story of the Bungalow Courts in Amarillo is a good illustration. In his postcard order he told the artist not to present the motel as being out on the prairie with nothing around it. "You might show some Lombardy Poplars," he wrote. The artist added the trees.

That's why *Portrait of Route 66: Images from the Curt Teich Postcard Archives* is important. We know the image the city or the business owner wanted to project, but the reality could be much different. By shedding light on the production process and, most importantly, offering the original photos for comparison, Baker's work and the Curt Teich archives are an invaluable resource to historians and nostalgia buffs. You might say they help us get the real picture of a time when getting there was half the fun.

PREFACE

EDITORS CHARLES E. RANKIN AND JAY DEW at the University of Oklahoma Press prompted me to put this book together, and I thank them for their insightful recommendation. We met during the fall of 2012, after I had made an extended research trip to the Chicago area. There among other efforts I had spent a week in the reading room at the Lake County Historical Society outside suburban Wauconda, Illinois. At the archival facility on the scenic grounds of a former dairy, I had discovered a visual resource that proved to be far more intriguing than I could ever have imagined.

The Lake County Historical Society holds the surviving archives of Curt Teich and Company of Chicago, once the largest postcard publisher in the United States. This is the only such archival collection from a postcard maker in the country, and the depth and breadth of the holdings is almost overwhelming. The Teich company printed quite literally hundreds of thousands of postcards over its seventy years of operation, and the production files survive for about 40 percent of the cards issued during its heyday, from the mid-1920s to the late 1950s. Many of the files include the original black-and-white photographs that customers provided as the raw material for Teich artists, who created color postcards before the widespread use of color photography.

I discovered photographs of eating places, motels, tire stores, and other business places and attractions that lined twenty-five hundred miles of former U.S. 66 across eight states. By the first morning I was photocopying photos and production file materials representing all these types of sites, and I did the same every day for the rest of the week. Throughout the process archivist Heather Johnson and her colleagues did everything possible to make the work thorough and efficient. By the time I finished, I had a stack with about fifteen hundred pages of photocopies. This pile of paper constituted a heretofore unknown raw portrait of the Mother Road.

On a visit to the University of Oklahoma Press in the fall of 2012, with a few of the photocopies spread out on a big conference table, editor Chuck Rankin asked, "T.L., why don't you put together a book using these pictures?" We discussed the pros and cons for a few minutes, and then he, Jay Dew, and I set to work picking out the images that comprise the current book. Quickly we decided that the work should include both the original photographs and the postcards made from them, both of which were available in the Teich

Collection. The combined judgments of a historian and two editors selected the images that we jointly thought were most representative of U.S. Highway 66 between the 1920s and the late 1950s. Soon production manager Emmy Ezzell got roped into the project as well.

One of the most enjoyable aspects of preparing this book was a field trip that my wife, Julie, and I made along the former U.S. Highway 66 looking for the places shown on the photographs reproduced from the Curt Teich Collection. We took the train from Texas to Chicago in July 2014, where we picked up a rental car at Union Station and drove the full length of the two-lane twenty-five hundred miles across the nation to Los Angeles. (About 85 percent of the historic pavement remains drivable.) We had with us a stack of photocopies of the historic photographs that had been selected for the book, and all along the way we sought out their locations on the ground. In the process we met multiple owners of the historic properties, most of whom had no notion that the historic photos existed. Sometimes we found only foundations or ruins of a building, but most of the time we were able to go to the very places where the photographs were made. This inspection led to the notes on the current status of the locations that accompany many of the captions. On our return by train from Los Angeles, we departed from its Union Station, an extraordinary building that has changed very little since its photograph in the book was taken in 1939. What a send-off that gave us! I thank Julie for her partnership in this research travel and for her encouragement and editorial assistance throughout the project.

During the preparation of this book, librarians and archivists, property owners and managers, and local experts have made significant contributions. Among these generous people along former U.S. Highway 66 and farther afield have been the following individuals: David G. Clark and Mark Mandle, Chicago; Heather Bigeck, Joliet, Illinois; Beverly K. Jensen, Dwight, Illinois; Tim Dye and Dave Sullivan, Pontiac, Illinois; Christie Huskins, Lincoln, Illinois; Joe Sonderman, Adele Heagney, Jay Buck, Elsey Hamilton, and Patrick W. Hensley, St. Louis; Don Fink, Eureka, Missouri; John F. Bradbury, Rolla, Missouri; Rosalie Klein, Lebanon, Missouri; Joan Hampton-Porter, Springfield, Missouri; Deborah Harvey and Michelle Hampton, Carthage, Missouri; Leslie Simpson, Joplin, Missouri; Scott Nelson, Riverton, Kansas; Jim Hall and Phyllis Abbott, Baxter Springs, Kansas; Barbara Becker, Miami, Oklahoma; Jennifer Holt, Claremore, Oklahoma; Sheri Perkins, Tulsa, Oklahoma; Bob Blackburn, William Welge, and Brett Sundstrom, Oklahoma City, Oklahoma; Penny Beals, Pat Reuter, and Carolyn Barker, El Reno, Oklahoma; Masel Zimmerman, Texola, Oklahoma; Larry Clonts, Shamrock, Texas; Delbert Trew, Alanreed, Texas; Warren Stricker, Canyon, Texas; Greg Smith, Bob Brinkman, and John Miller Morris, Austin, Texas; Dan K. Utley, Pflugerville, Texas; John McCall, Coppell, Texas; Mark E. Young, Houston, Texas; Debra Whittington and Joy Young, Tucumcari, New Mexico; Rhonda Brewer, Pecos, New Mexico; Ed Pulsifer, Santa Fe, New Mexico; Debra Slaney, Albuquerque, New Mexico; Dale Underwood, Gallup, New Mexico; Paul

Milan, Grants, New Mexico; Allan Affeldt, Winslow, Arizona; Al Richmond, Andrea Dunn, and Shirley Young, Williams, Arizona; R. Sean Evans, Flagstaff, Arizona; Charlotte Lindemuth, Seligman, Arizona; LaDawn Dalton, Prescott, Arizona; Jackie Snyder and Debbie Rusk, Kingman, Arizona; Joan Meis-Wilson, Needles, California; Hugh Brown, Essex, California; Larry Mikkelsen and Karen Everrett, Victorville, California; Sue Payne, San Bernardino, California; Carol Kampe, Monrovia, California; Sid Galley, Dan McLaughlin, and Anuja Navarre, Pasadena, California; Olivian Cha, Los Angeles, California; and Susan Lamb and Scott Albright, Santa Monica, California. Undoubtedly some of the places recorded in these historic photographs will change over time and my current descriptions will become outdated. I am certainly responsible for all the errors.

This remarkable historic portrait of the American roadside survives because of the shared desire of the Curt Teich heirs and the Lake County Historical Society in creating the Curt Teich Postcard Archives to preserve this extraordinary visual legacy. The greatest acknowledgment must go to them.

PORTRAIT OF
ROUTE 66

INTRODUCTION

IN MY PARENTS' HOME I FOUND a rectangular cardboard shoebox filled with picture postcards that I had collected on vacation trips during the 1950s. Like many thousands of Americans, I gathered these handy-sized color pictures of places I visited or hoped someday to see, or received them from friends and family members who were away from home. The images show a world beyond my small central Texas hometown, a world full of exciting things to experience. Because the cards were valuable to me, as an adolescent I safely put this shoebox away in the closet, where I discovered it decades later. Among the summertime trips they record was one we took in 1956 along parts of U.S. Highway 66 through the desert Southwest. Through these cards I recall the oppressive summertime heat and the scratchy mohair-upholstered back seat of a non-air-conditioned 1950 Mercury as our family crossed the Mojave Desert at night when the temperatures were the "coolest."

In the 1950s Route 66 was one of the most important cross-continental arteries connecting the eastern United States with the Pacific coast. It came into existence in 1926, when the federal government gave existing roads between major cities official highway numbers. The most important east–west thoroughfares were designated with two-digit multiples of 10, like 30 and 50. Promoters hoped the diagonal way between Chicago and Los Angeles would be given number 60, but in a compromise it received 66 instead. These "highways" in reality were pieced-together assortments of paved, gravel, and dirt roads. By the time the United States entered World War II in 1941, most of Route 66 had received concrete or asphalt. Much of the route consisted of simple two-lane pavement with no shoulders.

The highway began in Chicago, almost on the shores of Lake Michigan, and proceeded southwesterly for hundreds of miles. Along the first part of the drive, motorists passed endless cornfields; Abraham Lincoln's home at Springfield, Illinois; and then St. Louis, where the Missouri River joins the great Mississippi. The pavement led on through hills and vales of the green Ozarks, clipped through thirteen miles of southeastern Kansas, and thence on to Tulsa's Art Deco downtown, a testament to its oil boom days. Here on the banks of the Arkansas River, Highway 66 turned westward and maintained this direction all the way across the American Southwest. It proceeded over rolling, sometimes wooded red hills to Oklahoma City and onto the Great Plains, where the trees diminished in size and number until they disappeared completely in the flat Texas Panhandle. Beyond Amarillo to the west, the land gradually grew drier and then became desert, the bleakness punctuated by scattered intervals of trees in higher elevations that captured moisture from the clouds. This same occasional precipitation sometimes laid snow and ice on the roadway. The only real city on this stretch of two-lane was oasislike Albuquerque, watered by the Rio Grande. Motorists continued across the deserts and occasional high-elevation forests of Arizona, crossing the Colorado River into California and eventually passing into nature's oven, the Mojave Desert. After climbing the Cajon Summit, the roadway dropped down into a semi-tropical paradise beyond San Bernardino, where it passed miles of orange groves and rows of eucalyptus trees lining the pavement into Los Angeles and on to the Pacific shore at Santa Monica. Few highways in America could offer travelers such geographical and cultural diversity.

Route 66 travelers took to the road for all types of reasons. They might be headed to a family reunion just down the way or a wedding in another state. Some local motorists merely headed to the county seat to sell produce or shop for groceries and see a movie. Others traveled to a job or the hope of employment in some distant location. Many families headed out in hopes of escaping drought, unemployment, debts, or scandal. World War II attracted men and women to work in defense plants or to be near loved ones at military bases. As numbers of automobiles increased, more families left home for pleasure trips to destinations like Meramec Caverns or the Petrified Forest. There were seemingly as many reasons for people to set forth as there were individual motorists.

This road across the heartland of America constituted a real challenge for drivers. The easternmost stretches between Chicago and St. Louis offered reliable pavement, drainage, and signage. From the Mississippi Valley westward, however, driving conditions became unpredictable. For many miles the narrow road literally hugged the hills, giving motorists the feel of going up and down on gentle roller coasters, while passing slow-moving vehicles became hazardous maneuvers. Every stretch of Route 66 had its own "bloody curve" or "dead man's elbow." Wintertime ice and snow presented obvious complications. Distances were great, and many weary drivers tried to make the maximum number of miles in any given day. Drifting off to sleep at the wheel often led to death from head-on collisions or rollovers into ditches. In the days before safety glass, even minor accidents could result in dreadful lacerations from flying pieces of plate glass broken from car windows. Just changing a flat tire at the edge of the pavement with no shoulder could become a life-threatening operation.

The movement of thousands of Americans on highways like U.S. 66 created corridors of consumption where drivers could find the necessities of travel. Local residents viewed the motorists as new customers for gasoline, food, lodging, and repairs. As soon as the drivers began arriving in small communities, residents opened filling stations, diners, and tire-repair shops. Towns established free auto campgrounds for travelers, and cabins, tourist courts, and motels followed. Other enterprises, such as grocery stores, drugstores, and hotels, gained unexpected business because the cars brought them extra customers. In remote areas of the Southwest, enterprising businesspeople even constructed gasoline stations, cafés, and trading posts where there were no towns, in order to serve the cross-country travelers along lonely stretches. Impresarios opened the first truck stops to provide fuel and often the services required by long-haul drivers. An entire commercial subculture arose to serve the needs of highway motorists.

Another set of entrepreneurs discovered that motorists represented a completely new pool of customers for local natural attractions. They opened up otherwise forgotten underground caverns, graded dirt roads to volcano cones and meteor craters, and erected concession stands and picnic areas next to swimming holes and pretty groves of trees. If there were not already appealing natural features, some enterprising businesspeople created their own attractions by gathering collections of snakes or alligators and opening their own "reptile farms."

The heyday of travel on U.S. Highway 66 stretched from the 1920s to the 1960s. As early as 1956, however, President Dwight D. Eisenhower initiated creation of the interstate highway system. Modeled after the autobahns of Germany, these were multilane, restricted-access motorways that connected major cities and went around most towns. During the 1960s and 1970s these interstates gradually took the place of the old federal highways like number 66. Some of them remained in use as secondary roads, and some were abandoned. About 85 percent of old Route 66, for example, remains drivable as city streets, county roads, and state highways, while some other stretches are covered over by more modern pavement of interstates.

But an unexpected thing happened. Unlike most highways replaced by interstates, people along historic U.S. Highway 66 brought it back to life. In 1987 a barber whose shop fronted on the old road in Seligman, Arizona, began a grassroots movement that eventually led to the creation of state-level Route 66 associations in each of the eight states along the old road to promote recognition of its historical significance. Soon tourists started seeking out the old pavement to drive the historic roadway for themselves. Author Michael Wallis published the "Bible" of the roadies, *Route 66: The Mother Road*, in 1992 and thereby encouraged the nostalgic movement to preserve the old highway and its roadside culture. Since that time more and more property owners and others along the historic highway have repaired, restored, and interpreted multiple elements of the historic roadside landscape, including pavement, bridges, and old-time places of business. Today probably as many tourists from abroad take "the California trip" along the old road as do travelers from the United States, with *Air France Magazine* declaring former U.S. Highway 66 to be "the largest open-air museum in the world."

Many of the current Route 66 roadies collect postcards of the Mother Road the same way I did as a kid. They go from stop to stop, looking for the miniature views on cardstock on which they can send messages. Some of them seek out and pay premium prices for the old postcards as well, trying to find all the vintage cards from the highway in a particular state or maybe collect just motel postcards. Few of the collectors, however, know very much about the original photographs "behind" each of those views.

Picture postcards as we know them came onto the American scene in 1907. Up to this time the U.S. Post Office Department had required that postcards have the address on one side and the written message on the other, leaving no space for pictures. But in March 1907 it began to allow the "divided back" postcard, with an address and a written message on one side and an illustration on the other. Almost immediately publishers began producing postcards with pictures on one side and space on the other for brief messages, postage stamps, and addresses. A craze struck the nation: for a few years both young people and adults went into a frenzy of mailing postcards to each other. Many of these greetings ended up in albums where they survived in remarkable condition. Some cards bore amusing cartoon pictures, others showed reproductions of paintings, and yet others, prepared on photographic paper, were actual black-and-white photographs. Among the most popular were printed postcards illustrating scenic landscapes, cultural attractions, and urban street

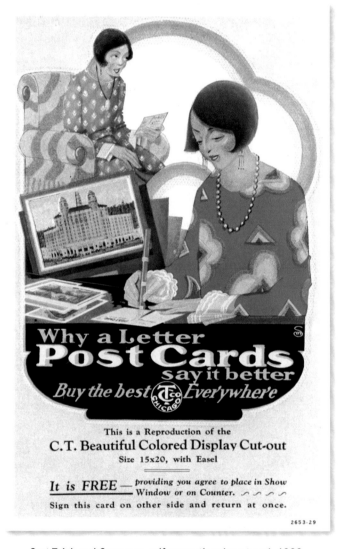

Curt Teich and Company, self-promotional postcard, 1929.

scenes. Using a variety of printing processes, the pictures on the postcards generally were rendered in color. Over the years a number of companies eventually produced millions of these inexpensive picture postcards.

One of the premiere postcard makers operated in Chicago. Founded in 1898 by an immigrant from Germany who had grown up in a family of printers, Curt Teich and Company grew to become one of the largest producers of postcards in the United States. It is best remembered today for popularizing "linen surface" cards, on which the picture side had a texture reminiscent of linen fabric. Using three different halftone printing processes, the company produced cards with distinctively bright colors and frequently high-quality graphics. Until the company closed in 1978, it printed postcards showing views of almost every town in America, including communities along U.S. Highway 66 from end to end.

After receiving an inquiry from a prospective customer, clerks at Curt Teich and Company responded by sending out basic order and price information. Purchasers learned that postcards were comparatively cheap: in 1935 they cost between $8.00 and $12.50 per thousand on orders of 6,000, or 0.8¢ to 1.25¢ apiece depending on the printing process. The

Curt Teich and Company Plant, self-promotional postcard, 1932.

Postcard production file for the Rest Haven Motor Court, Springfield, Missouri, 1951–52. For more information—including the raw photographs and the finished postcard—see pages 54–55.

company directed buyers to submit original clear black-and-white photographs measuring five by seven or eight by ten inches. The firm also advised clients to lay sheets of translucent tissue paper on top of the photographs and to draw outlines with pencils on the tissue overlays to identify which subject matter should be printed in which colors based on about thirty choices available on enclosed charts. Some clients requested colors that differed from reality to make their cards more appealing. At this stage buyers also made requests to delete unwanted subject matter in the photographs, like utility poles or people. They might even go so far as to ask company artists to add trees where there were none or to render partly cloudy skies out of overcast.

When an order arrived in Chicago at the Teich printing house, a clerk assigned it a production number and placed the materials in a large brown envelope. He pasted a summary of the order on the outside of this production file and rubber-stamped it with a chart for recording production progress. Graphic artists then created the postcard design. This might consist of an unaltered original photograph, a retouched photo with painted or airbrushed enhancements, or original images rendered in tempera-like paint. At this point the technician prepared a full-color sketch the size of a postcard that went to the customer for approval. Once the printer received the customer's comments, the technician prepared a printed proof that included any wording to appear on the front or back. It, too, went to the customer for acceptance. When the client gave the second authorization, the card went into production. After the cards were printed and shipped to the buyer, Teich employees put away the production file so that it would remain available for reference should the customer order any future reprints of the same card. Today about 40 percent of the production files for Curt Teich postcards from the mid-1920s to the 1960s survive. Some of these job jackets contain original photographs, letters, and other order materials, while others consist only of empty envelopes with order summary and the production checklist on the outside.

Curt Teich and Company was sold in 1974, and the plant closed in 1978. Teich's family wanted the records of the firm to be preserved, but had difficulty finding an archive willing to accept such a large donation of business papers. The massive collection included examples of over 360,000 different postcards plus commercial records, postcard-finding aids, and surviving production files. Finally a home was found at the Lake County Historical Society in Wauconda, Illinois, not far from Curt Teich's suburban home. There the collection has been catalogued and for several years has been made accessible to on-site researchers.

It was in the production files from Curt Teich and Company that I located the photographs and associated postcards that comprise this book. While searching for historic photographs depicting eating places along former U.S. Highway 66, I found instead a treasure trove of original photographic images documenting the full range of roadside attractions and enterprises. Two editors at the University of Oklahoma Press and I selected the images that fill the pages that follow. Though they are seldom used by scholars, original historic photographs comparable to these are available in the Curt Teich Archives for approximately ten thousand different communities in North America.

With these photographs and the postcards that were based on them, the reader is invited to travel back to the days when U.S. Highway 66 served as a key artery of commerce connecting the United States. Most of the way was two-lane pavement lined with mom-and-pop business enterprises like Ed Wright's tire shop in Tulsa, Oklahoma, and Roy's Free Camp Ground in Kingman, Arizona. Through these pictures, readers can relive a time when cars had no air-conditioning, many tires were made from natural rubber, and motorists struggled to get their vehicles up and down the switchbacks at Sitgreaves Pass in Arizona. Thanks to the customers of Curt Teich and Company, we can enjoy views of the Mother Road that we would never otherwise get to see.

Featured Locations along Route 66

ROUTE 66

ILLINOIS

1 Conrad Hilton Hotel, Chicago
2 Berghoff Restaurant, Chicago
3 Greyhound Bus Terminal, Chicago
4 Morton's Restaurant, Chicago
5 Cocktail Lounge, Hotel Louis Joliet, Joliet
6 West Main Street, Dwight
7 Phoenix Hotel Restaurant, Pontiac
8 Pontiac Café and Service Station, Pontiac
9 Greyhound Post House, Pontiac
10 S. S. Kresge Company Building, Lincoln

MISSOURI

11 Club House *Piasa*, Harbor Point Marina, West Alton
12 The Dome Cocktail Bar, St. Louis
13 Buckingham's Restaurant, St. Louis
14 Sylvan Beach Park and Restaurant, St. Louis
15 Bridge Head Inn, Times Beach
16 Pennant Hotel, Rolla
17 Trav-L-Odge, Rolla
18 U.S. Highway 66 Bridge over the Gasconade River, near Waynesville
19 Commercial Street, Lebanon
20 Rest Haven Motor Court, Springfield
21 Rock Village Court, Springfield
22 Lampe-Birkenback Garage, Storage, and Service Station, Springfield
23 Tourist Park, Carthage
24 Boots Court, Carthage
25 Dick & John's Bar, Joplin
26 Junge Baking Company Animated Billboard, Joplin
27 U.S.O. Club, Joplin
28 Holiday Inn Ballroom, Joplin

KANSAS

29 Main Street, Galena
30 Tourist Camp, Galena
31 Travelers' Inn, Galena
32 Spring River Bridge, near Baxter Springs
33 Main Street, Baxter Springs

OKLAHOMA

34 Sooner State Motor Kourt, Miami
35 Will Rogers's Birthplace, near Chelsea
36 Hotel Will Rogers, Claremore
37 Ed Wright Tire Company, Tulsa
38 Beverly's Chicken in the Rough, Oklahoma City
39 Beverly and Rubye Osborne with Their Chicken in the Rough Western Girls, Oklahoma City
40 Garland's Drive-In Restaurant, Oklahoma City
41 El Fenix Restaurant, Oklahoma City
42 McDonald-Scott Chevrolet Company, Oklahoma City
43 El Charro Café, Oklahoma City
44 Skirvin Hotel, Oklahoma City
45 Venetian Room, Skirvin Hotel, Oklahoma City
46 Herman's Restaurant, Oklahoma City
47 Patrick's Drive-In Food, Oklahoma City
48 Phillips Courts, El Reno

TEXAS

49 Oldham's State Line Station, East of Shamrock
50 Shamrock Court, Shamrock
51 Pueblo Court, Amarillo
52 Pueblo Court and Station, Amarillo
53 Smith's Motel, Amarillo
54 Longchamp Dining Salon, Amarillo
55 Bungalow Courts, Amarillo
56 Old Tascosa Room, Herring Hotel, Amarillo
57 The Aristocrat Restaurant, Amarillo
58 Cunningham Floral Company, Amarillo
59 Sunset Motel, Amarillo

NEW MEXICO

60 Aerial View of Tucumcari
61 U.S. Highway 66 through Tucumcari
62 Two Bridges on the Pecos, Santa Rosa
63 Oldest Well in U.S.A., Glorieta Pass
64 La Fonda Hotel, Santa Fe
65 The Patio, La Fonda Hotel, Santa Fe
66 The Indian Room, La Fonda Hotel, Santa Fe
67 Guest Room, La Fonda Hotel, Santa Fe
68 F. W. Woolworth Company Building, Santa Fe
69 La Bajada Hill, between Santa Fe and Albuquerque

ARIZONA

78 La Posada Hotel, Winslow
79 Passageway to West Wing, La Posada Hotel, Winslow
80 The Lounge, La Posada Hotel, Winslow
81 The Santa Fe *Super Chief*, near Flagstaff
82 Kaibab Motor Lodge, Williams
83 Havasu Hotel, Seligman

ILLINOIS

MISSOURI

KANSAS

OKLAHOMA

TEXAS

CALIFORNIA

92 Front Street, Needles
93 El Garces Hotel, Needles
94 Bender's One Stop Super Service Station, Amboy
95 Southwest on Main Street, Ludlow
96 Northeast on Main Street, Ludlow
97 Desert Inn Hotel, Ludlow
98 Street Scene, Victorville
99 Third Street, San Bernardino
100 Leven Oaks Hotel, Monrovia
101 Francois French Restaurant, Pasadena
102 Arroyo Seco Parkway, Los Angeles
103 Clifton's Pacific Seas Cafeteria, Los Angeles
104 Aloha Stage, Clifton's Pacific Seas Cafeteria, Los Angeles
105 Waiting Room, Union Station, Los Angeles
106 Earl Carroll Theatre-Restaurant, Hollywood
107 Beverly Hills Hotel and Bungalows, Beverly Hills
108 The Miramar, Santa Monica
109 Belle-Vue French Café, Santa Monica
110 Club del Mar, Santa Monica
111 Beach at Club del Mar, Santa Monica
112 O. J. Bennett's Sea Food Grotto, Santa Monica

70 U.S. 66 Four-Lane Highway through Tijeras Canyon, East of Albuquerque
71 Alvarado Hotel, Albuquerque
72 KiMo Theater, Albuquerque
73 Indian Silversmiths from Maisel's Indian Trading Post, Albuquerque
74 Katson's Drive-In, Albuquerque
75 Fourth of July Parade, Grants
76 El Navajo Hotel, Gallup
77 The Lobby, El Navajo Hotel, Gallup

84 Kerby's Auto Camp, Seligman
85 Bird's-Eye View of Peach Springs
86 Main Street, Peach Springs
87 Peach Springs Trading Post, Peach Springs
88 O. C. Osterman Auto Court, Peach Springs
89 Roy's Free Camp Ground and Service Station, Kingman
90 City Café and Texaco Station, Kingman
91 Colorado River Bridge, Topock

PONTIAC CAFE AND SERVICE STATION ON ROUTE 4, CHICAGO TO ST. LOUIS, PONTIAC, ILL.

4387-29

CHAPTER ONE

ILLINOIS

U.S. HIGHWAY 66 BEGAN near the lakefront in downtown Chicago, at the intersection of Jackson Boulevard and Michigan Avenue. After one-way streets were introduced, its westbound start shifted one block north, onto Adams Street. This was a skyscraper district where businessmen stayed in lodgings such as the Conrad Hilton and the Palmer House and dined in places like the Berghoff Restaurant and Miller's Pub. The unassuming roadway extended westward and southwestward past the landmark Union Station and Lou Mitchell's Restaurant, where people still savor the special French toast, and on into residential neighborhoods. From there the highway proceeded on four-lane streets via Cicero and outlying suburbs into farm and dairy country through tidy towns like Joliet and Dwight.

Soon the Illinois landscape changed from urban housing to rural fields. Its summertime stalks of corn grew more than head-high. Motorists took rest stops in places like the City Café in Pontiac or the soda fountain in the O'Malley and Stitzer Drugstore in Dwight. The roadway cut through the natural wonder of an isolated maple forest on an otherwise treeless prairie at Funk's Grove. The travelers drove on to the state capital at Springfield, passing the impressive domed capitol building, and some made the pilgrimage to Abraham Lincoln's home and mausoleum or paused to sample freshly fried corn dogs at Ed Waldmire's Cozy Dog Drive-In.

By the 1940s the thoroughfare between Chicago and St. Louis was paved with concrete, two lanes each direction, so travelers could speed along between the two great cities. The pavement made broad loops around many of the communities along the way. The situation ahead would be far different for early drivers in many states, such as Texas, New Mexico, and Arizona, where the first pavement was only being contemplated. Nevertheless, motorists in the Midwest enjoyed smooth going except during the wintertime, when ice and snow might impede travel and even paved Route 66 became treacherous.

As the Mother Road gradually descended into the immediate valley of the Mississippi River southwest of Edwardsville, travelers encountered more traffic congestion. Industrial enterprises lined the sides of the great river that drains much of North America, and metropolitan St. Louis lay just ahead on the other side. Some motorists with a little time diverted to Spencer A. Atkins's stern-wheel riverboat, which had been converted to a floating restaurant and party venue in an inlet along the Mississippi just upstream from St. Louis, while others sped on to find lodging for the night or a nice meal on Italian Hill in the city itself.

Conrad Hilton Hotel

CHICAGO, ILLINOIS

1952

The Conrad Hilton Hotel, now the Hilton Chicago, fronts on Michigan Avenue four blocks south of the beginning of Route 66 at Michigan and East Jackson Boulevard. Constructed in 1927 as the Stevens Hotel, the twenty-nine-story facility for many years held the distinction of being the largest hotel in the world.

James Stevens, who had made a fortune running the Illinois Life Insurance Company, was joined by his sons in building the Stevens Hotel on the Chicago lakefront. The opulent facility was almost a city unto itself, having its own rooftop miniature golf course, theaters, bowling alley, and multiple restaurants. Guests entered through the main entrance doors on the front, each surmounted by a giant stylized S. Hard economic times, however, were not far away: the Black Tuesday stock market crash would occur only two years later. Eventually son Ernest was tried for embezzling insurance company funds to help keep the hotel afloat, though the conviction was reversed by the state supreme court. The family struggled to retain ownership of the hotel and eventually sold it to the federal government during the Second World War to serve as housing and classrooms for trainees in the U.S. Army Air Corps. The Grand Ballroom, scene of elegant soirees, for a while became a giant mess hall.

After the war the army sold the huge building to a local businessman who in turn sold it to Conrad Hilton and his Hilton Hotel Corporation. In a major project, the company renovated the entire facility into a luxurious mid-twentieth-century hotel. It added a giant ice stage to the Boulevard Supper Club to feature elaborate ice-skating shows. Remaining part of the Hilton chain, the hotel received an even more extensive update during the mid-1980s, when the 3,000 guest rooms were reconfigured as 1,544 larger and more comfortable chambers. The name changed to the Chicago Hilton and Towers, later the Hilton Chicago, though the large letter S for Stevens remains in bronze above the main entrance doors on Michigan Avenue.

In spring 1952 the Hilton Hotel Corporation in Chicago ordered a remarkable five hundred thousand color postcards from Curt Teich and Company based on this photograph. Employees at the printing house began the production process on May 19, 1952, giving the printing job stock number 2C-H726. The first fifty thousand cards were due for delivery to the customer within twenty-five working days, with the balance to follow.

THE BOULEVARD ROOM

THE
Conrad Hilton
CHICAGO, ILLINOIS

Berghoff Restaurant

CHICAGO, ILLINOIS

1952

The Berghoff Restaurant at 17 West Adams Street is two blocks from the start of Route 66 in downtown Chicago. It is a landmark, and not just for travelers. For decades it has been a mecca for lovers of German food and German beer.

Herman Joseph Berghoff, an immigrant from Dortmund, Germany, in 1887 founded a modest brewery in Fort Wayne, Indiana. He managed to get a concession to sell his beer to fairgoers at the 1893 World's Columbian Exposition in Chicago, and from that springboard in 1898 he opened a saloon and eating place on West Adams Street in the Windy City. He sold beer to his patrons and offered free sandwiches and other foods to increase business, which continued until the start of national prohibition in 1919.

Berghoff switched to bottling nonalcoholic near beer and soft drinks, adding a full-service restaurant to supplement his business. When Prohibition ended in 1933, Berghoff's received City of Chicago Liquor License No. 1, a distinction it continues to hold each year. Since 1933 customers have enjoyed Berghoff's distinctive Dortmund-style German beer.

Food, however, is still a major attraction at the Berghoff, which for decades has operated at 17 West Adams Street, one door down from its original 1898 location. In 1931 food writer John Drury proclaimed, "Pig's knuckles and sauerkraut, Thueringer sausage and red cabbage and other such heavy Teutonic dishes [are] served appetizingly in this old landmark on the Loop." Modern food critics Jane and Michael Stern have written rhapsodically about Berghoff's "meat-and-potatoes meals . . . with a German accent," like pot roast served with noodles "glistening with butter."

The Berghoff Restaurant Company in Chicago ordered twenty-five thousand color postcards based on these photographs. The paperwork with the photos enclosed must have reached Curt Teich and Company by October 9, 1952, for on that day its staff gave the job stock number 2C-P2531 and began the printing process.

Right to 5"
2CP2531

Greyhound Bus Terminal

CHICAGO, ILLINOIS

1953

Many of the travelers on Route 66 chose to take the Greyhound bus rather than drive. The Greyhound Corporation became the largest of the interstate motor coach firms, though it did not have a single large terminal in Chicago until the 1950s. As early as 1941 the company began planning a large new terminal to take the place of its two separate stations. It acquired the western half of a city block bounded by Randolph, Clark, Lake, and Dearborn Streets in the north end of the Loop area in the central city, but then the rationing of strategic materials during World War II made it impossible to secure the materials needed to construct the facility.

In the summer of 1949 tenants began vacating the last buildings at the proposed Greyhound terminal site, with demolition following. Construction soon began on a projected five-story bus station, two levels of which would be underground. The sub-basement became the bus-loading concourse, capable of handling thirty-one motor coaches at the same time. Above it but below street level were the main waiting room, ticket offices, and other passenger services shown in the picture. At ground level a third concourse surrounding the open space above the waiting room housed thirteen retail stores that opened both inside and outside to the sidewalk. Above these areas were two levels of automobile parking for bus customers and others. Six escalators moved people conveniently from level to level.

The Greyhound Bus Terminal served Chicago travelers for almost forty years. During the 1980s the company was already planning construction of a replacement terminal that would be nearer to the major railway stations. By this time deferred maintenance was taking its toll on the building. Chicago Route 66 historian David Clark remembered, "It was a dump." Consequently the terminal moved to a new facility located more conveniently for travelers just a few blocks from Union Station, the arrival point for Amtrak passenger trains.

The Aero Distributing Company of Chicago ordered twenty-five thousand color postcards showing the interior of the new Greyhound Bus Terminal based on this artwork created by Curt Teich illustrators and copied from a photograph. Production began on April 22, 1953, when the printing house staff assigned the job stock number 3C-H565.

241—Interior View of New
Greyhound Bus Terminal, Chicago

© CURT TEICH & CO., INC.

Morton's Restaurant

CHICAGO, ILLINOIS

1951

Morton's Restaurant became one of the dining landmarks in the Hyde Park area, on the south side of Chicago, from the 1930s to the 1950s. Mort Morton initially began the enterprise as a saloon at the end of Prohibition in 1933. When the commercial space next door became available, he enlarged the operation and added food service. By the early 1950s the combined eating and drinking establishment at 5487 South Lake Park Avenue occupied the ground levels of two adjacent three-story apartment buildings. A sign across the front in neon tubes and incandescent bulbs spelled out "Morton's an Adventure in Good Eating." This location not far from Lake Michigan could be easily accessed by motorists via South Lake Shore Drive from the head of Route 66, about six and a half miles to the north.

Mort Morton, his sons, and other family members expanded their restaurant business in the mid-1950s, opening Morton's Surf Club at the site of the old Palm Grove Inn about six blocks east of the old eatery at the extreme end of East Fifty-Sixth Street on South Lake Shore Drive. That larger restaurant, managed by son Eddie Morton, specialized in barbecued ribs but also offered all the standard dishes, including steaks, chicken, chops, and seafood.

Another of Mort's sons, Arnold J. Morton, born in 1922, became famed in Chicago for his culinary achievements. With others he cofounded the Playboy Club in 1959; he was the partner responsible for food and drinks. He later established a series of other bars, restaurants, and nightspots, among them the notable Morton's Steakhouse on North State Street. This eatery opened in 1978 and later became the basis for the creation of the international chain of restaurants called "Morton's: The Steakhouse." Chicagoans remember Arnie Morton most especially as the founder of the annual "Taste of Chicago" summer food festival, which began in 1980.

Morton's Restaurant ordered twenty-five thousand postcards printed in green from Curt Teich and Company based on several photographs; the printing company assigned the job stock number D-9808 on May 8, 1951.

Luxury in Privacy—for Group Meetings

Distinctive Dining—Quiet, Pleasureful

Cocktail Lounge, Hotel Louis Joliet

JOLIET, ILLINOIS

1942

Constructed in 1927, when hotels were still the most popular overnight lodgings in the United States, the Hotel Louis Joliet was for decades the largest and most luxurious hostelry in Joliet, the first real city that Route 66 motorists encountered after leaving Chicago. Named for the seventeenth-century French explorer of the upper Mississippi, Louis Joliet, the city prospered into the 1920s due to factories, steel mills, proximity to the Illinois and Michigan Canal, access to multiple railway lines, and state operation of a major prison.

Urban hotels during the 1920s were more than just places where people found overnight lodging. Their rooms for business meetings and social functions and their establishments serving food and beverages became the places where major deals were made for the exchange of goods and services. The eight-story brick and stone Hotel Louis Joliet, one of the largest structures in downtown Joliet, for years played this important role in the city's economic and social life.

In 1926 local real estate promoter Fred J. Walsh and others organized the Clinton Square Hotel Corporation to raise funds in the amount of $750,000 to build the Hotel Louis Joliet. Construction began later that year. The U-shaped, eight-story structure, which was made of reinforced concrete, brick, and stone and had 225 guest rooms, opened in August 1927. Its location at 22 East Clinton Street was only half a block east of the 1926 alignment of U.S. Highway 66 through Joliet along North Chicago Street. It shared a block with the 1926 Rialto Square Theater, regarded by some as one of the ten most beautiful theaters in the world.

The hotel prospered during the late 1920s but suffered economically during the Great Depression. By the time the photograph of the cocktail lounge was taken about 1942, the hotel had entered three and a half years of full occupancy and profitability during World War II. It slipped back into the doldrums again during the 1950s and 1960s due to competition from outlying motels and a general decline in the central city. The Active Order of Carmelites of the Aged and Infirm purchased the building in 1964, converting it to a residence for the elderly, a role it continued to serve until its much more recent purchase and rehabilitation, when it became the Historic Louis Joliet Apartments.

The Hotel Louis Joliet itself ordered twenty-five thousand color postcards from Curt Teich and Company based on this photograph. Employees assigned the job stock number 2B-H983 on September 12, 1942.

Cocktail Lounge
HOTEL LOUIS JOLIET
JOLIET · ILLINOIS

West Main Street

DWIGHT, ILLINOIS

1928

Druggists John O'Malley and Laurie Stitzer wanted a postcard to show their business in the 100 block of West Main Street in Dwight, Illinois, a village located eighty miles southwest of Chicago. In so doing they associated their building with its prominent neighbors to the northeast, the Frank L. Smith Bank and the Keeley Institute.

In 1905 Dwight businessman Frank L. Smith, in partnership with others, established the bank. He hired a budding architect, Frank Lloyd Wright, to design their building, a story-and-a-half stone structure with strong horizontal and vertical elements. Opened in 1906, the bank continues serving the community as the First National Bank over a hundred years later. In the photograph its building is covered with vines. Thousands of heritage tourists driving on Route 66 stop off each year to view this early commission by the internationally known architect.

Farther down the street, to the right, stand two masonry buildings with columns. They formed part of the complex of the Keeley Institute, a well-known center established by Dr. Leslie Keeley in 1879 for the treatment of alcoholism. Together with later franchised facilities in more than two hundred other locations in America and Europe, the Keeley Institute assisted people suffering from alcoholism with treatments that included multiple daily injections of biochloride of gold and other substances. The institution closed in 1965, but these buildings currently form part of the W. W. Fox Developmental Center, operated by the Illinois Department of Mental Health.

O'Malley and Stitzer played their own role in the history of Dwight. John O'Malley purchased a small drugstore in the town in 1911 and then was joined by Laurie L. Stitzer as a partner in 1919. By the 1920s the two men had built the enterprise into one of the largest drugstores in Livingston County. The emporium offered not just medications but also stationery, sundries, tobacco, confectionery, and even ice cream and beverages at a soda fountain. The property was cleared about 1990 to make way for construction of a drive-up window at the bank next door.

Curt Teich and Company received a request from O'Malley and Stitzer in Dwight for one thousand black-and-white postcards showing the 100 block of West Main Street. Employees at the printing house received the materials by September 27, 1928, on which date they assigned the job stock number 122896 and began production. At the customer's request, Teich artists slightly retouched the photograph to "take off chimney" and "show lettering—O'Malley & Stitzer Drugs."

West Main Street, Dwight, Ill.

122896

Phoenix Hotel Restaurant

PONTIAC, ILLINOIS

1927

Because they attracted out-of-town attorneys, clients, and others during legal proceedings, courthouse squares became prime locations for hotels during the nineteenth century. Before the arrival of railroads these hostelries often doubled as stagecoach inns for passengers. This was the case of the Union Hotel, constructed south of the Livingston County Courthouse at Pontiac in 1871. Its builders could not have predicted that their almost-new structure would burn, together with adjoining buildings, in a fire ignited by Independence Day fireworks only three years later, on July 4, 1874. Built quite literally on top of the ashes, the three-story brick Phoenix Hotel rose just months later. When U.S. Highway 66 was designated in 1926, its initial route through Pontiac passed directly by the hotel. The facility provided lodging for travelers for almost a century; it closed in 1973 and was razed the next year.

As the principal downtown hostelry in Pontiac, the Phoenix Hotel provided food service for both travelers and local residents. Its location at the heart of the commercial district almost guaranteed customers, and the restaurant on its Washington Street front offered a full range of meals. In 1943 the name of the inn changed from the Phoenix Hotel to the Pontiac, by which time it offered a formal dining room as well as a cocktail lounge. Specialties of the house included tender steaks, southern-style fried chicken, homemade potato pancakes with applesauce, and, according to its ads, fresh-baked pies "like Mother used to make, only better."

The management of the Phoenix Hotel contacted Curt Teich and Company to order one thousand black-and-white postcards showing its restaurant. The mailing reached the printing company by August 15, 1927, when its clerks assigned the job stock number 116023.

PHOENIX HOTEL RESTAURANT, PONTIAC, ILL.

116023

Pontiac Café and Service Station

PONTIAC, ILLINOIS

1929

The location of Pontiac, Illinois, on Illinois State Highway 4 between Chicago and St. Louis brought the town a substantial flow of north–south motorists even before the 1926 routing of U.S. Highway 66 through its downtown district. By the 1920s the community abounded with roadside enterprises that supplied the needs of both locals and traveling motorists. Among the most common were gasoline filling stations and eating places.

Built in 1926–27, the Pontiac Café and Service Station was one of these early road-related businesses. Located directly on U.S. Highway 66 at the corner of North Ladd and West Madison Streets, the enterprise initially sold Deep Rock Gasoline from gravity-type pumps and served meals featuring barbecue, steaks, and pork chops. Green- and ivory-painted stucco covered the exterior, while green- and gold-striped fabric awnings shaded some of the windows. Gasoline customers could drive right up to the pumps on the sidewalk for convenient fueling.

As Pontiac's commercial district grew, the needs changed for the land on which the Pontiac Café and Service Station were built. By 1940 the stucco commercial building at 749 West Madison became a neighborhood grocery store operated by individuals including Clyde F. and Viola P. Cramer, Joseph Acklin, and Jimmy Hicks, and it served this function for decades. The structure survived until about 1980, when it was removed and a new building erected that at the time of writing housed an insurance office.

In the fall of 1929, the owner of a variety store in Pontiac named Fritz Bolander ordered thirty-five hundred color postcards based on this retouched photograph from Curt Teich and Company. He instructed the printer to show an American flag atop the building but to remove a wooden utility pole that would have obscured the left side of the view. The printing job reached Chicago by October 11, 1929, when Teich staff gave it stock number 4387–29. Eighteen days later the Great Depression began with the Black Tuesday stock market crash.

PONTIAC CAFE AND SERVICE STATION ON ROUTE 4, CHICAGO TO ST. LOUIS, PONTIAC, ILL.

4387-29

Greyhound Post House

PONTIAC, ILLINOIS

1940

As travel by bus increased in volume in the late 1930s, it did not take long for the old downtown Pontiac bus station, sharing space inside a café, to become inadequate. The depot shifted from there to another location at 342 North Mill Street, but that facility also presented limitations. Consequently the Greyhound Corporation decided that the town on U.S. Highway 66 deserved to have its own proper motor coach station. The Post House Restaurant inside provided meals and a rest stop for bus passengers at the midpoint between Chicago and Springfield.

Greyhound originated in 1914 through the efforts of Swedish immigrant Carl Wickman, who built the firm into the largest intercity motor coach service in America. By 1927 Greyhound buses were transporting passengers from New York to California. Although the company suffered during the first years of the Great Depression, by 1935 it was again earning profits in the millions of dollars. Soon Greyhound was erecting multiple new bus stations across the country, most of them in the iconic style popularly called Streamline Moderne, which emphasized long horizontal lines and curving forms.

When in 1940 the Greyhound Corporation erected its new terminal at 420 North Plum Street at its intersection with West Livingston Street, west of downtown Pontiac, the handsome masonry structure with a rounded cornice, a flat roof, and industrial steel windows epitomized Streamline Moderne styling. The facility provided waiting rooms, a ticket office, a parcel express, a café, and support areas for travelers. After serving the traveling public until 1961, the building eventually found alternative use as a physician's clinic and as the local driver's license office. At the time of writing, it housed the Livingston County Community Pantry. Although the upright "Greyhound" sign is missing from the front of the former station, the decorative curved cornice still preserves the historic feeling.

The Greyhound Corporation in Chicago ordered five thousand black-and-white postcards based on this photograph showing its newly erected station in Pontiac. The job reached Curt Teich and Company by July 27, 1940, the day when its employees assigned it stock number D-6381.

GREYHOUND POST HOUSE
PONTIAC, ILLINOIS

S. S. Kresge Company Building

LINCOLN, ILLINOIS

1951

The most valuable property in downtown Lincoln, Illinois, during the late nineteenth and early twentieth centuries fronted the Logan County courthouse square. The largest and most impressive commercial edifices sprang up along its northwest side, the 100 block of South Kickapoo Street, including the 1867 three-story brick Gillett-Oglesby Building. It offered retail space on its ground level, offices on the second floor, and the meeting hall and auditorium of the Masonic fraternal order on the third. Essayist Ralph Waldo Emerson is said to have given a lecture in the upstairs meeting space. This center of activities in Lincoln, owned by the family of Meyer Griesheim, burned to the ground in 1932 at a loss of about $100,000. Despite the economic stress of the Great Depression, his daughter and son-in-law rebuilt on the site without delay.

Agreeing to a long-term lease of the ground floor to the S. S. Kresge variety store chain, the family erected the handsome building featured on the Curt Teich and Company postcard. The contractor used light tan brick, Italian marble, and terra-cotta Art Deco ornamentation, which was fashionable and at the time was the Kresge firm's favored style. For years the "five-and-dime" store operated on its lower level, with additional tenants upstairs. Subsequently the edifice provided space for other commercial enterprises. The Kresge Building still survives, and so does the entire block of historic buildings shown in the photograph. They stand to this day as attractions for present-day heritage tourists traveling Route 66.

S. S. Kresge Company in Lincoln sent an order for thirty-five hundred color postcards to Curt Teich and Company based on this west-facing photograph composed to show its store in the corner of the 100 block of South Kickapoo Street. The job went into production in Chicago when Teich employees gave it stock number 1C-H478 on October 12, 1951.

South Kickapoo Street—Main Business Section, Lincoln, Illinois

THE GEM OF THE OZARKS

COMMERCIAL STREET, LEBANON, MO.

1449-29

CHAPTER TWO

MISSOURI

ST. LOUIS SERVED AS THE GATEWAY TO THE WEST, where wagon trains provisioned, during much of the nineteenth century. In the next century it became the gateway to Missouri on Route 66. Westbound motorists entered the state as they crossed the Mississippi River bridges from Illinois. Many travelers tarried in St. Louis and dined on its specialties, such as toasted ravioli, gooey butter cake, or chicken dinners at Buckingham's Restaurant. Others drove on through the big city to relax on the banks of the Meramec River at scenic retreats like Sylvan Beach, a resort on the west side, or at the Bridge Head Inn, a little farther on at Times Beach.

Travelers found Missouri to be a state of green rolling hills and the beautiful Ozark Mountains. Westward from St. Louis, Highway 66 passed through hilly areas with deep valleys, all covered by dense forests. Travelers passed through Lebanon and cultivated fields, seeing the land change from hilly to rolling. By the time drivers reached southwestern Missouri, the landscape became only gently rolling, with trees concentrated mostly along streams and the borders of fields.

By the middle of Missouri, visitors started noticing increasing numbers of houses and other buildings ornamented with exterior veneers of flat, variegated brown stones. Many roadside businesses like filling stations, cafés, and tourist courts employed this attractive construction material. Because the irregular pattern in the stones resembled the spots on African giraffes, some people called these Ozark stone buildings "giraffe houses." The area along the 66 Highway between Springfield and Joplin, Missouri, abounded with this construction; typical examples included the Trav-L-Odge in Rolla and the Rock Village and Rest Haven motels in Springfield.

Springfield considers itself the "birthplace of Route 66." It was here in 1926 that highway planners proposed the compromise of designating the federal highway linking Chicago with Los Angeles with number 66, and the number stuck. It is believed that the meeting took place in highway promoter John T. Woodruff's office building, located just behind the Lampe-Birkenback Garage in Springfield.

As motorists proceeded southwest, they entered the Tri-State Mining District, an important center of lead production for the entire United States. The mineralized area began in southwestern Missouri and extended westward into Kansas and southwestward into Oklahoma. In some areas the waste from the historic mines formed giant heaps of tailings that created moonscapes of poisoned soil. Joplin, through which U.S. 66 passed, became the largest of all the urban centers serving the mining area.

Club House
Piasa,
Harbor Point
Marina

WEST ALTON, MISSOURI

1953

Spencer A. Atkins of St. Louis was one of many people who at one time owned this paddle-wheel steamboat. He had the money to afford such a luxury because of his family's successful businesses. His grandfather founded the first large drug company in St. Louis, and his father became its president. On returning home from serving as the youngest U.S. Army major during World War I, Spencer built his fortune in fuel oil, river barge operation, and agriculture. In 1940 the impresario purchased a naturally sheltered anchorage on the west bank of the Mississippi River near the community of West Alton, Missouri, just north of St. Louis. He resided there, where his Harbor Point Boat and Dock Company operated a marina. The location near the U.S. Highway 67 bridge over the Mississippi made it easily accessible to motorists traveling on the nearby Route 66.

In 1948 Atkins purchased the used stern-wheel steam-powered towboat originally built in 1921 as the *Mamie S. Barrett*. The Howard Shipyard had launched it on the Ohio River at Jeffersonville, Indiana. The U.S. Army Corps of Engineers purchased the steamboat in late 1923 and for the next twenty-four years used it on inland waters, renaming it the *Penniman* in 1935. In 1942 the agency added an elevator and a special bathtub so that President Franklin D. Roosevelt could use the vessel for an inspection of the Mississippi River. Army engineers in 1947 decommissioned the steam towboat, which the next year went into the hands of Spencer Atkins. He adapted the time-worn vessel into a floating restaurant for his marina, giving it the new name *Piasa*. It even took diners on short excursions on the Big Muddy under steam. In time its power equipment was removed and the boat was floated to Eddyville, Kentucky, and later to Vicksburg, Mississippi; in both places it functioned as a floating theater and bistro. It was next towed to Vidalia and then to Deer Park, Louisiana, where at the time of writing it lay beached and gradually deteriorating. Spencer Atkins's Harbor Point Marina on the Mississippi River serves today as a residential development with docks primarily for pleasure craft. The site is about eight miles upstream from the Mississippi's juncture with the Missouri River.

Spencer Atkins's Harbor Point Boat and Dock Company ordered one thousand black-and-white postcards from Curt Teich and Company to be made from this photograph of the old *Mamie S. Barrett* steamboat being reused as the *Piasa* floating restaurant. Its mailing reached Chicago by April 22, 1953, when printing house staff gave it stock number 3C-183.

5⅛ Square

6¹¹⁄₁₆

CLUB HOUSE "PIASA" — HARBOR POINT MARINA

The Dome Cocktail Bar

ST. LOUIS, MISSOURI

1940

The Dome Cocktail Bar is one of a series of retail establishments that over the years conducted business on the ground floor of the Silk Exchange Building on the north side of downtown St. Louis. The building where the Dome operated was erected in 1902 in the garment district. It housed small-scale clothing and millinery manufacturers, as well as agents for clothing, lace, fabric, buttons, and notions produced elsewhere. It was Morris Woolf's 1907 Silk Exchange Realty Company that gave the building its name. The street level at various times provided commercial rental space for restaurants, a corner cigar store, and saloons, and later for bars.

The Dome Cocktail Bar does not appear in St. Louis city directories until 1942, although it clearly was in operation in the fall of 1940, when its managers placed an order for Teich postcards. Operators of the bar listed in city directories from 1942 through 1946 were John B. Howard, John L. O'Connor, and Harry L. Delgman. The 1946–47 volume notes only Howard and O'Connor. The last known reference to the Dome shows up in the 1949 St. Louis telephone directory. By 1952 the city business guide listed the South Seas Cocktail Lounge at 511 North Twelfth Street, the location of the former Dome.

Manufacture of clothing during the mid-twentieth century moved from the United States to foreign countries with cheaper labor costs, and the entire garment district in St. Louis declined. By the early 1980s the Silk Exchange Building was vacant, and in 1995 the unoccupied structure suffered a major fire that led to its demolition. At the time of writing, its former site was green space bounded on three sides by Washington Avenue, North Tucker Boulevard (formerly North Twelfth Street), and St. Charles Street.

The Dome Cocktail Bar ordered sixty-five hundred color postcards based in part on this photograph from Curt Teich and Company by October 4, 1940, the day the company gave the order stock number 0B-H1946.

The *Dome*

AIR CONDITIONED

511 NORTH 12th STREET
ST. LOUIS

Buckingham's Restaurant

13

ST. LOUIS, MISSOURI

1946

Throughout America owners of large, aging houses fronting on busy thoroughfares sometimes adapted them to commercial use. This happened to a vacant two-story bungalow with shingle cladding at 8945 Manchester Road on the west side of St. Louis, Missouri. An entrepreneurial couple converted the home into a restaurant that soon attracted a loyal clientele of both travelers and local residents.

By 1943 Clyde C. and Mabel "Trixie" Ann Buckingham had established an eating place in a handsome former residence on the north side of U.S. Highway 50. (The roadway had carried Route 66 traffic east and west as early as 1926, but its alignment shifted about four miles south to Watson Road in 1933.) Known as Buckingham's, it was described by American food critic Duncan Hines in 1949 as "largely a chicken dinner restaurant—fried and baked—but they also serve T-bone steaks, Swiss steaks and fried shrimp." He added that it specialized in "home-type food, including pies and rolls." One local resident remembered, "An uncle took my grandmother there at least once a month back in the '40s and '50s." Multiple large rooms in the house made it ideal for bridge clubs and special parties, while air-conditioning kept the interior comfortable during muggy St. Louis summers.

Mr. and Mrs. Buckingham operated the restaurant into the early 1960s, when they sold the enterprise to Bennett J. and Sue Barton, who continued the business under the Buckingham name until about 1969. By the next year a business management service had moved into the facility, after which possession passed to a real estate broker. At the time of writing, Hensley Construction, Inc., occupied and maintained the building. Currently painted white, the handsome old home stands in the municipality of Brentwood, Missouri, at the slightly altered street address of 8949 Manchester Road, between Brentwood Boulevard and High School Drive.

Curt Teich and Company received an order from Buckingham's Restaurant for 12,500 color postcards based on this photograph. The packet of materials reached Chicago by February 20, 1946, when printing house employees gave it stock number 6B-H202.

COMPLETELY AIR CONDITIONED

BUCKINGHAM'S — 8945 MANCHESTER ROAD, (U.S. 50) — ST. LOUIS, MO.

Sylvan Beach Park and Restaurant

ST. LOUIS, MISSOURI

1946

14

On the Meramec River west of St. Louis, Sylvan Beach occupied one of the most desirable places for local recreation. River currents endangered bathers along most of the waterway, but a gravel bar at Sylvan Beach made it one of the few locations where people could swim in safety. Easy auto access at the Route 66 bridge helped to create an ideal setting for outdoor leisure-time activities.

In 1932 landowners Frank and Ethel L. Wiemeyer leased the property fronting on the east bank of the river and north of U.S. Highway 66 to Louis Peters and his partners. The investors built a restaurant, swimming pool, baseball fields, picnic facilities, and bridle paths along the river near the roadway, creating a weekend playground for city dwellers. Perhaps the group overextended itself financially, as it went bankrupt by 1935, during the depths of the Great Depression. Mr. and Mrs. Wiemeyer took over the private amusement area, and under their management it began turning a profit.

An unexpected attraction at Sylvan Beach Park was a quarter-mile dirt racetrack for midget racing cars that opened in 1936. Styled like regulation Indianapolis racers, the miniature vehicles had small gasoline motors but no starters or roll bars. Typically the owners built them from kits. Members of drivers' pit crews pushed the little racers to start their engines, while audience members sat in open-air bleachers cheering their favored speedway contenders on.

Sylvan Beach Park and its restaurant operated until 1954, when the Missouri Highway Department erected a pair of new bridges to carry U.S. Highway 66 traffic across the Meramec River. This construction absorbed part of the area formerly occupied by the restaurant and recreational facilities. The swimming pool continued to operate for a few years, and eventually became the Kirkwood city pool, even though it was inside the municipal bounds of Sunset Hills. At the time of writing, most of the former Sylvan Beach Park that had escaped being obliterated by the highway expansion was encompassed by the Emmenegger Nature Park, and an old neon sign from the Sylvan Beach Restaurant could be seen on exhibit at the Route 66 State Park at Times Beach, near Eureka, Missouri.

By June 6, 1946, Curt Teich and Company received an order from Sylvan Beach Park for twenty-five thousand composite color postcards, to be made in part from this photograph. The job went into production with stock number 6B-H950.

Sub for Picture Under "The Spot"

SYLVAN BEACH PARK
and RESTAURANT
St. Louis - Missouri

Bridge Head Inn

TIMES BEACH, MISSOURI

1939

Along the eastern third of Route 66, motorists frequently patronized "road houses." These usually rural establishments, akin to old-time stagecoach inns, provided meals for travelers, together with beer and, frequently, stronger drinks and dancing. The Bridge Head Inn on the Meramec River at Times Beach, about sixteen miles west of St. Louis on U.S. Highway 66, was just such a place.

In 1925 a St. Louis newspaper began promoting the area along the Meramec as Times Beach, a scenic retreat for city residents. The community grew into a scattering of rural homes and weekend cottages served by a variety of eating and drinking establishments, the nicest of which was the 1935 Bridge Head Inn. Later becoming Steiny's, the Bridge Head Inn again, and finally the Galley West, the establishment served meals and beverages for almost fifty years.

Times Beach grew to about two thousand residents by 1972, when a contingent prevailed on town authorities to spray the unpaved streets with oil to reduce dust. Little did anyone realize that the petroleum put down by the Russell Bliss Asphalt Paving Company was laced with high levels of cancer-causing dioxin. The firm made a business of removing chemicals and oil from industrial facilities and then disposing of the waste by laying the toxic sludge on the dirt streets of unsuspecting communities. In 1982 the federal Environmental Protection Agency (EPA) announced that the streets of Times Beach were so filled with poison that everyone would have to leave the town. Eventually the EPA purchased the entire site; removed every building except the Bridge Head Inn, which became its administrative center; and burned over 250,000 tons of dioxin-contaminated soil in a massive cleanup.

By 1997 the EPA had completed cleaning up Times Beach and turned the site over to the Missouri Department of Natural Resources. Because former U.S. Highway 66 traversed part of the former community, the state adapted it to a new purpose: it is now the Route 66 State Park, and the old Bridge Head Inn serves as the park's headquarters and interpretive center. Thousands of heritage tourists and others visit the state park each year, learning not only about the Mother Road but also about how ignorance and greed effectively killed the town of Times Beach.

The Bridge Head Inn ordered two thousand "varicolor" postcards to be printed in dark blue and vermilion. The mailing reached Curt Teich and Company by March 28, 1939, when its employees assigned the job stock number D-5779.

DINING ROOMS

TAP ROOMS

BRIDGE
HEAD
INN
★
TIMES BEACH
EUREKA, MO.
★

Highway 66 — 16 Miles West of St. Louis

Pennant Hotel

ROLLA, MISSOURI

1931

Henry Clay Pierce, president of the Pierce Petroleum Company, admired Fred Harvey's concept of clean, well-managed hotels and eating places for railway travelers. He thought so much of the idea that he decided to build similar institutions to serve motorists.

When the U.S. Supreme Court decreed that John D. Rockefeller's Standard Oil Trust must be dissolved, the Waters Pierce Oil Company split into several parts, one of which was the Pierce Petroleum Company. Henry Clay Pierce lost control of the firm in 1925, but his successor, Edward D. Levy, took up Pierce's objective of "abandoning 'shanty' service stations for architecture and convenience."

Both Pierce and Levy envisioned a chain of Colonial Revival–style "taverns" that provided fuel, food, and lodging every 125 miles on major highways. They also planned to construct full-service filling stations with superior restrooms about midway between each of the larger taverns. The company started in the Ozarks with the first Pierce Pennant Tavern at Springfield, Missouri, in July 1928; the second one opened in Rolla on 1 August the same year. On November 1, 1929, a four-story Pierce Pennant Hotel followed on a nearby hilltop fronting on the Mother Road on the north side of Rolla. Timing was bad for such an ambitious project: the U.S. stock market crashed on October 29, 1929, three days before the hotel's opening ceremonies in Rolla. With sales dwindling as the economic depression deepened, the Pierce Petroleum Company in 1930 sold to the Sinclair Consolidated Oil Corporation.

The imposing Pierce Pennant Hotel, however, continued serving travelers at Rolla for decades. Ownership changed over the years: the venerable hotel operated for a time as the Sinclair Pennant Hotel and later as the Carney Manor. The facility narrowly avoided destruction when an expanded four-lane U.S. Highway 66 was built in the 1950s, but then was demolished to be replaced by a modern Drury Inn at 2006 North Bishop Avenue atop the same commanding hilltop.

Local drugstore owner John W. Scott in Rolla ordered one thousand "blue sky" postcards from Curt Teich and Company based on this photograph. These otherwise black-and-white cards had the sky overprinted in light blue. The paperwork reached Chicago by February 5, 1931, when the job received stock number 1A345.

SINCLAIR PENNANT TAVERN, ROLLA, MO.

1A345

Trav-L-Odge

ROLLA, MISSOURI

1950

Along the highways across America, entrepreneurs during the 1920s and 1930s built roadside lodgings for travelers. These affairs often began as simple campgrounds for tents and canvas flies, but soon resourceful operators added simple furnished cabins. The lodgings often reflected local construction practices, and in Missouri and Oklahoma this included the use of characteristic multihued brown stone veneers.

Throughout the Ozark Mountains, through which Route 66 passed in Missouri, Kansas, and Oklahoma, both limestone and sandstone abound. This sedimentary rock can easily be split into large, flat pieces, and during the 1910s skilled builders started using these to create decorative veneers on building exteriors. Stonemasons laid out the flat stone pieces on the ground, shaping them where necessary to ensure a close fit. Then they smeared mortar on the exterior walls of the buildings and stuck the flat pieces of stone in place in visually random patterns. The variegated brown shades of the irregular stones reminded folks of a giraffe's hide, so the structures came to be known as giraffe houses. If other types of stone were available, like rubble or river-washed cobbles, the masons used them likewise for decorative effect. The Trav-L-Odge tourist court in Rolla had buildings constructed using both giraffe-pattern stone and rubble masonry.

At least as early as 1939 Bernard Stair erected two tourist cabins at what he called the Trav-L-Odge, on property at the north side of Rolla fronting on U.S. Highway 66. That same year he sold the property to Mr. and Mrs. W. E. Reed, who then transferred ownership to their daughter, Jessie Maude Mundis. She took possession, managed operations, and expanded the tourist court. After her health declined, Mundis rented the court to others, among them O. W. Dickerson, Roy Lochrie, and William O'Havre.

The World War II years seem to have been profitable. The Trav-L-Odge offered multiple units for overnight lodging and opened its own Trav-L-Odge Steakhouse. An article in the local press in 1945 described the café as "one of Rolla's most popular eating places." Proximity to a huge U.S. Army training camp at Fort Leonard Wood boosted Trav-L-Odge business. After the war the motel continued serving Route 66 travelers but changed its name to the Rolla Motel, and the restaurant became a Chicken in the Rough franchise. The motel operated until about 1975, when all the buildings were razed and the site redeveloped for a filling station–convenience store that at the time of writing occupied the site in the 1900 block of North Bishop Avenue.

On November 16, 1950, Curt Teich and Company in Chicago received a request for 12,500 color postcards based on this photograph, which was retouched to enhance some of the details. The card went into production with stock number 0C-H1891.

title in Sky

Signs in line for black

$5\frac{9}{16}$ Comb.

TRAV·L·ODGE
ROLLA, MISSOURI

U.S. Highway 66 Bridge over the Gasconade River

NEAR WAYNESVILLE,

MISSOURI

1954

The Gasconade River is the longest watercourse within the bounds of Missouri. It begins in the Ozark Mountains near Hartville and flows north-northeasterly 240 miles before emptying into the Missouri River. Inspired by the swiftly churning waters of the river, early French settlers named it after people originating in the French province of Gascony, known for their enthusiastic natures. For much of its length, the stream passes through eroded meanders and beneath impressive bluffs in the Ozarks.

Erecting bridges across a major river like the Gasconade was taken seriously. This was certainly the case in 1922, when engineers from the Missouri Highway Commission planned a bridge on the main road between Rolla and Springfield. They used a combination of two Parker truss spans, one Pratt truss span, and one open-top Warren truss span supported on reinforced-concrete piers and abutments, giving the bridge an impressive total length of 526 feet.

A truss consists of two long, roughly horizontal chords linked together by both vertical posts and diagonal elements. On the Gasconade River Bridge, these components are all steel beams. Trusses employ the strength of triangles: some members compress toward each other, while others pull apart. When properly designed, as in the case of this bridge, the parts distribute stress through the entire truss to bear its own weight and that of vehicles passing over its roadway.

The Illinois Steel Company in Chicago, Illinois, fabricated the metal pieces for the Gasconade River Bridge according to plans drawn by engineers at the Missouri State Highway Department. Then the Riley and Bailey Construction Company built the concrete piers and abutments and assembled the steel truss structures on top of them. Erection began in 1922, and the bridge went into service in 1924; the total project cost $70,273.40. With brief interruptions for repairs and maintenance, the bridge served the public for ninety years, and until the Interstate 44 spans were erected downstream in the 1950s it was the only highway crossing over the Gasconade in this part of the state. In December 2014 the Missouri Department of Transportation announced that the old Route 66 bridge on the access road alongside the interstate would be closed indefinitely due to lack of funds for repairs or replacement.

The Corwin News Agency in Jefferson City, Missouri, placed an order for 12,500 color postcards showing an aerial view of the U.S. Highway 66 bridge across the Gasconade River. The materials reached Curt Teich and Company by November 22, 1954, on which date employees gave it stock number 4C-360 and began production.

U. S. Highway 66 Bridge over Gasconade River
in the Scenic Missouri Ozarks

Commercial Street

Lebanon, Missouri, always has been on arteries of travel. Even before there was a town, a trail created by the Wyota and Osage Indians traversed the area. It was followed in the 1860s by an Anglo-American trace that came to be called the "Wire Road" after the telegraph line at its side connecting Springfield, Missouri, with St. Louis. Then came the St. Louis–San Francisco Railway in 1868. Local landowners had refused to grant the company a free right-of-way, prompting the railroad to locate its station a mile south of the existing town center. Most businesses relocated to the "new town" alongside the railway; many of them erected buildings on Commercial Street, which paralleled the rails. In 1926 U.S. Highway 66 became the next connection to link Lebanon with the rest of the world, followed by Interstate 44.

Milan W. Searl, a druggist operating a shop at 125 West Commercial Street, was part of a water company that in 1887 made a discovery that for a while brought notoriety to Lebanon: workers employed by the company found that water from a well they had drilled actually magnetized the steel tools they were using. Searl began selling "magnetic water" to health seekers who came to Lebanon to drink and bathe in the waters. He managed the drugstore until about 1896, when he sold to John McMillen and a man named Manning. Emmet Milsap later purchased Manning's share in the enterprise, and he stayed on in partnership with McMillen and then ran the shop on his own for over a quarter century. The initial drugstore building eventually was replaced with another two-story brick structure that at the time of writing housed a nail salon.

It was druggist Emmet Milsap who wanted to sell postcards showing downtown Lebanon. To this end a photographer stepped out onto the rain-slickened 100 block of West Commercial Street, pointed his camera southwest toward the intersection with South Madison Street, and snapped the shutter. The location was about six blocks northwest of historic U.S. Highway 66 on Elm Street.

Milsap's Drug Store sent this photograph to Curt Teich and Company as the basis of an order for thirty-five hundred color postcards. It reached the printer and received stock number 1449–29 on March 30, 1929. Although the picture was taken on an overcast, rainy day, the Teich artists rendered the image on the card to show bright, partly cloudy weather.

THE GEM OF THE OZARKS

COMMERCIAL STREET, LEBANON, MO

1449-29

Rest Haven Motor Court

SPRINGFIELD, MISSOURI

1951

Hillary Brightwell became a Route 66 businessman in 1936, when he left a Depression-era job for the Works Progress Administration and relocated to Springfield, Missouri. There he bought a small White Rose gasoline station on the west side of town, but he had trouble selling enough fuel to make a living. Although he priced his gasoline reasonably at 10.9 cents a gallon, most customers typically had the money for only two or three gallons at a time. "I didn't do much business," he confessed, so he sold the station. He then managed another on the opposite side of Springfield near the junction of U.S. 65 and U.S. 66. During World War II in 1942 he married and became a family man.

After the close of the war, the couple purchased the gasoline station. "In 1947, we decided to build some motel units," Hillary remembered. Behind the station they erected a row of four Ozark stone-veneer cottages each with two guest rooms, but it was not easy. Wartime shortages persisted, and it was difficult even to find necessities like bathroom fixtures. Once the cabins were finished, they put up a sign calling the lodging Rest Haven. Their location near the important road intersection brought business, and in 1952 the Brightwells added ten more rooms in a row across the rear, and then another ten rooms on the second side three years later. In 1953 they put up a handsome neon and incandescent sign; they also disassembled the old filling station and reconstructed it in the rear as a storage building. In time the couple remodeled the individual cottages into a continuous motel, filling in the spaces between the units with additional rooms.

A major change came with the rerouting of U.S. Highway 66 in 1958. To stay competitive after the diversion of traffic to the north, the Brightwells added a swimming pool in the open space at the center of the motel and then placed sidewalks and porches in front of the rooms. They managed the lodging until 1978, when they retired and sold Rest Haven to their successors. At the time of writing, the motel remained in operation serving the traveling public. It has become a destination for many heritage tourists seeking the experience of staying in vintage overnight accommodations on the Mother Road.

On September 26, 1951, Curt Teich and Company received a request from the Rest Haven Motor Court for 12,500 composite color postcards. The mailing included these two photographs of a room interior and the gift shop. Printing house employees assigned the job stock number 1C-H1360 and began production.

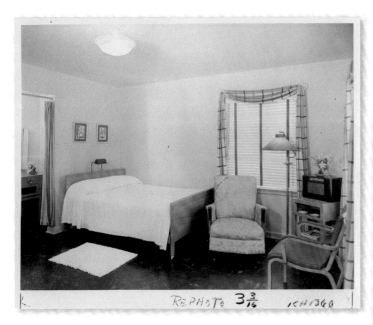

REST HAVEN
MOTOR COURT
AAA
E. 66
SPRINGFIELD, MISSOURI

Rock Village Court

SPRINGFIELD, MISSOURI

1950

The 1947 Rock Village Court at the intersection of U.S. Highways 66 and 65 in Springfield, Missouri, is another example of design self-expression. This motel and restaurant combined smooth and rounded Streamline Moderne architectural style with thin slabs of native Ozark stone as decorative veneer. Fashionable glass blocks admitted natural light throughout the complex. Advertising promoted Rock Village Court as "one of the finest and most beautiful courts" in the country, calling it "an unusually picturesque group of native stone and glass brick cottages and hotel."

Travel and food writer Duncan Hines recommended Rock Village, pointing out its convenient location near the major highway junction about two and a half miles east of downtown Springfield. He reported that the motor court was open year-round and offered its guests steam-heated rooms with radios and tiled combination tubs and showers. A double room in 1950 rented for five to seven dollars a night, so this was not a cheap place to stay.

In addition to its cottages, Rock Village also made available several hotel-style rooms in its main building. On the ground level of this structure was a coffee shop called the Dogwood Dining Room, which was noted during the 1950s for its tasty meals served with special sorghum whipped butter.

Renovated over the years, Rock Village Court survived into the 2000s as the Solar Inn. At the time of writing, a recently built America's Best Value Inn occupied its location at 2355 North Glenstone Avenue.

On January 12, 1950, an order from the Rock Village Court arrived at Curt Teich and Company for twenty-five thousand composite color postcards showing three views of the motel. The two photographs reproduced here accompanied those materials and survived in the production file number 0C-H96, which began on that date.

Lampe-Birkenback Garage, Storage, and Service Station

SPRINGFIELD, MISSOURI

1930

As urban areas grew in size and numbers of automobiles exploded during the 1920s, it became increasingly difficult for drivers to find convenient places to park their cars. Astute investors consequently erected downtown multistory garages to create the needed spaces to park cars while people worked, shopped, and dined at city centers.

Springfield, Missouri, businessmen Grover Lampe and Milton W. Birkenback saw this opportunity in the late 1920s. Acquiring the site of a former church at the southwest corner of East Olive Street and North Jefferson Avenue, half a block from U.S. Highway 66, they erected a five-story reinforced-concrete building that housed a service station and garage on its lower level and space for three hundred motor vehicles on the upper floors. Faced with brick and stone, it simulated the appearance of surrounding offices and retail stores. The principal difference was that from inside emanated the nearly continuous squealing of rubber tires on the spiral concrete ramps between the floors. Over the years the businesses inside the building changed, giving the property such names as Lampe-Birkenback Garage, Lampe-Birkenback Auto Hotel, Miller Tire Company, and the Congress Garage. It operated until 1972, when the structure was razed and the site converted to surface parking.

The taller office building to the left rear of the parking garage in the photograph had its own particular connections with U.S. Highway 66. Erected by local real estate investor John Thomas Woodruff in 1911, the Woodruff Building became the setting for many important meetings in the history of Springfield. It was likely here that promoter Cyrus Avery, Missouri Highway Commission Chief Engineer B. H. Piepmeier, Woodruff, and other advocates of a cross-country highway between Chicago and Los Angeles met on April 30, 1926, to resolve several questions about its routing and identification. In this gathering the participants settled on the number 66 for the new highway and proposed it to the U.S. Bureau of Roads, giving Springfield the distinction of becoming the "Birthplace of Route 66."

On May 17, 1930, Curt Teich and Company received an order from the Lampe-Birkenback Company for 12,500 color postcards showing their parking garage in Springfield. Teich employees assigned it stock number A-2232–30, created a production file, and started the job.

Garage, Storage, and Service Station

LAMPE-BIRKENBACK CO., Springfield, Mo.

2232-30

Tourist Park

CARTHAGE, MISSOURI

1930

Years before Route 66 came to Carthage, the town served as a stop on the Jefferson Highway, which connected Winnipeg, Manitoba, with New Orleans. Many long-distance drivers entered the community looking for places to camp or seek lodging. The town became well known to early auto campers as one of the best places to pitch tents for the night.

In 1897 Dr. John A. Carter donated approximately ten acres of land on the northeast side of Carthage for a city park. By the time Jefferson Highway motorists started arriving in the late 1910s, Carter Park was improved with shelters, fireplaces, and decorative stonework. When the grade of West Central Avenue in the town was lowered to facilitate passage beneath a railway line, the handsome stone entry shown in the photograph was moved to the park from its former location at the entrance to the Victorian-era Cassill Place residential development. With increased use by motorists, the open green space also came to be known as the Tourist Park.

In January 1922 the *Modern Highway* magazine described Carthage Tourist Park as having electric lights, shade trees, drinking water, showers, free firewood, and tables with benches. By 1926, when U.S. Highway 66 through Carthage received its numerical designation, travel writer Richard A. Martinson in *Everybody's Magazine* declared that Carthage Tourist Park was one of the two best such facilities in the entire United States. He praised its "cook-house with a battery of gas stoves, two eating pavilions of stone, sinks and running hot water, lights, and commodious shower rooms." For years the Tourist Park served auto campers in Carthage. In time it was supplemented by the privately owned Taylor Tourist Park and then by motor courts. Though it no longer serves as a public campground, as Carter Park on East Chestnut Street it still welcomes visitors to the Ozark community.

F. W. Woolworth's variety store in Carthage requested thirty-five hundred black-and-white postcards based on this photograph showing the Tourist Park. The order reached Curt Teich and Company by May 13, 1930, when it staff assigned the job stock number 2131–30 and started production.

TOURIST PARK, CARTHAGE, MO.

2131-30

Boots Court

CARTHAGE, MISSOURI

1945

Arthur Boots was a preeminent entrepreneur. Formerly in farm equipment sales, he relocated to Carthage in 1938 after studying road maps for a future motel location. He purchased a city lot near the intersection of Garrison Avenue with Central Avenue in Carthage, the place where U.S. Highway 66 (east–west) met U.S. 71 (north–south).

To generate at least some income, Boots erected a gasoline filling station at the east end of the lot fronting on Garrison about 1938. Then he constructed the motel in his own version of the fashionable Streamline Moderne style. It had a flat roof, rounded corners inside and out, white stucco wall surfaces, black glass and neon trim, and covered drive-through spaces that permitted guests to shelter their cars while parking directly in front of their rooms. Boots did most of the work himself, including laying up the masonry walls and fabricating metal frames for fabric-covered window awnings. Boots's son remembered that a plasterer named Shorty helped apply the stucco to exterior and interior walls.

The tourist court prospered so well that Arthur Boots removed the gasoline pumps and renovated the station at the front of the building into the motel office. About the same time he added four more guest rooms. His personal life, however, did not go so well, and he and his wife divorced in the early 1940s. She continued operating the motel, while Arthur in 1946 erected a Streamline Moderne drive-in restaurant directly across the street. Mr. and Mrs. Pleas Neeley purchased the motel in 1944, and two years later they added a row of five additional white stucco guest rooms at the rear. In time the motel suffered neglect, but then new preservation-minded owners took over in 2011 and began a thorough restoration of the iconic landmark known by thousands of Route 66 travelers. At the time of writing, five of the rooms have been fully restored to pristine 1940s condition and are available to lodge overnight guests, and work is under way on the rest of the historic hostelry. Carthage did not receive television service until about 1953, so the beautifully refurbished rooms offer entertainment from reproduction Crosley radio sets.

Boots Court itself ordered six thousand black-and-white postcards from Curt Teich and Company based on this photograph. The printer began production by assigning it stock number D-7950 on November 14, 1945.

title in plate   5 9/16   P   8

JUNCTION 66 AND 71 - CARTHAGE, MO.

Dick & John's Bar

JOPLIN, MISSOURI

1937

Before the enforcement of national Prohibition began in 1920, Joplin abounded with watering holes. Some of them were nightclubs with music, dining, and dancing, while others were just hole-in-the-wall bars. For thirteen years legitimate production and sale of beer, wine, and other alcoholic beverages ended, though many people disobeyed the laws. As soon as lawmakers repealed Prohibition in 1933, legal alcohol sales rebounded.

One of the Joplin businessmen who took advantage of the repeal was John Davenport, who with Dick Metsker in 1936 opened Dick & John's Bar. It operated in a long, narrow storefront commercial building with windows in the front at 636 Main Street. Early the next year they sent Curt Teich and Company an order for postcards showing their establishment crowded with customers. There are so many people in the picture, in fact, that one almost wonders whether they were offered free drinks just to come in and pose for the photographer.

Despite a location in downtown less than a block away from the last alignment of Route 66 along Seventh Street, Dick & John's Bar did not persist as an institution in Joplin. Davenport and Metsker described it as "swell" even though they offered customers, in their own words, "bad drinks, terrible foods, poor service, [and] rotten music." Within a year of its founding, Davenport had moved on to open John's Bar at 213 West Fourth. For the next quarter century he operated a series of Joplin taverns with such names as the Pla-Mor Bar, Kum-Bak Bar, Ringside Tavern, Sixty-Six Domino, and Mom's Rainbow Tavern. The building that housed Dick & John's was razed in the 1960s as part of urban renewal in the city center.

Dick & John's Bar placed an order for six thousand black-and-white postcards from Curt Teich and Company based on this photograph. Their paperwork reached Chicago by January 12, 1937, for on that day printing house employees gave it stock number D-4757.

merphos 5x7

"DICK and JOHN'S BAR" — 636 MAIN STREET, JOPLIN, MISSOURI — DICK METSKER and JOHN DAVENPORT, Proprietors

Junge Baking Company Animated Billboard

JOPLIN, MISSOURI

1940

The Walt Disney animated cartoon movie *Snow White and the Seven Dwarfs* took the United States by storm when it was released before Christmas in 1937. It was the first ever full-length animated feature film in motion picture history. During its initial release, *Snow White* grossed the highest income of any talking movie up to that time.

Throughout the United States companies took advantage of the appeal of the *Snow White* movie to sell products. The long-standing Junge Baking Company of Joplin, Missouri, as early as October 1938 marketed its own brand of "Snow White" sliced white bread in a waxed paper wrapping printed with pictures of Disney's dark-haired songstress and her companions.

During the mid-1930s the firm created a changeable billboard with moving parts in Junge Park, a green space adjacent to one of its bakeries at the northwest side of the intersection of West Nineteenth Street and South Main. The site was about a dozen blocks south of Highway 66 along Seventh Street. Custom artwork on this 22-by-65-foot three-dimensional "greeting card" welcomed each change in the seasons. The signboard featuring Snow White coincided with the company's 1938 promotion of the special Snow White brand of bread.

In summer 1940 the Junge Baking Company ordered 12,500 color postcards of the Snow White billboard. The mailing reached the printer by August 13, 1940, when it gave the job stock number 0B-H1376. It sent Curt Teich and Company two black-and-white photographs of the signboard in daylight and illuminated at night. Instructions called for the reverse side to read, "This talking, animated and illuminated sign is the only sign of its kind in the U.S.A. and possibly the world. On exhibition from sunset to 10 P.M. each night." Sadly, Junge Park, the location of the historic billboard, is no more; its site is occupied by a Hardee's restaurant at the time of writing.

ANIMATED ELECTRIC SIGN (Snow White and 7 Dwarfs)

AT THE HOME OF **JUNGE'S BAKERY PRODUCTS** • JOPLIN, MO.   0B-H1376

U.S.O. Club

JOPLIN, MISSOURI

1943

Joplin, Missouri, was a town founded on lead and zinc mining, but during World War II it was the largest urban center in proximity to Fort Crowder, a major U.S. Army training facility established about thirty miles to the southeast, near much smaller Neosho. The U.S. War Department created the post in 1941 to train armored troops, but in time the base also prepared signal corps replacements and housed an officers' candidate school. The base survived into the mid-1950s.

The influx of military trainees to Fort Crowder resulted in large numbers of young men making their way into Joplin looking for good times. As a former mining camp, the town offered an abundance of bars, taverns, and nightspots. Community leaders, however, wanted to give service personnel more wholesome options for recreation. They worked with the United Service Organization (U.S.O.) to open a leisure center in a preexisting commercial building at 310 Wall Street, just two blocks west of U.S. Highway 66 along South Main Street. There U.S.O. staff and volunteers staged dances, screened motion pictures, held summertime watermelon feasts, and hosted outings into the Ozarks.

Sponsors of the U.S.O. Club in Joplin, however, found themselves in an unexpectedly awkward situation when African American trainees began arriving at Fort Crowder. The customary racial segregation of the day prevented black service personnel from socializing with whites attending functions at the local club. After two years of inaction, local leaders opened a separate U.S.O. Club for blacks on the second floor of a building two blocks away at 221 South Main Street, directly on the Route 66. During wartime operation, the two Joplin U.S.O. clubs served an estimated one million Fort Crowder service personnel and their family members.

After the Second World War the structure at 310 Wall Street reverted to business use. At the time of writing, the commercial building was sheathed in cream-colored siding that disguised its appearance.

The Adams News Company in Joplin ordered 12,500 color postcards showing the white U.S.O. Club. Curt Teich and Company received the mailing by June 3, 1943, when its staff assigned the job stock number 3B-H715. The customer requested that the artists add an American flag at the sidewalk in front and remove an automobile parked at the right edge of the photograph. Many armed service members from around the country used these cards to write notes home to friends and family members.

straighten   3BH 715

Joplin U. S. O. Club, Joplin, Missouri

Holiday Inn Ballroom

JOPLIN, MISSOURI

1946

In 1942 dancer Fred Astaire and crooner Bing Crosby starred in a popular feature-length movie with music by Irving Berlin titled *Holiday Inn*. The film is best remembered today for introducing Bing's famous song "White Christmas." For several years thereafter ballroom dancing was associated with *Holiday Inn*. Aware of this connection, John R. Garrison about 1946 chose this as the name of his new ballroom at 3230 South Main Street in Joplin, Missouri.

During the 1920s and 1930s, ballroom dancing was all the rage among young Americans. They flocked to huge halls with hardwood floors to dance to the strains of such national band leaders as Tommy Dorsey, Paul Whiteman, and Glenn Miller, as well as regional counterparts. In 1936 the Dancing Teachers' Business Association claimed that six million Americans were taking lessons so they could waltz, foxtrot, tango, and two-step. Throughout the Great Depression dancing provided Americans with inexpensive and welcome diversion from personal and economic problems.

Shortly after the close of the Second World War, John R. Garrison constructed his impressive stone Holiday Inn Ballroom on the south side of Joplin. It was easily accessible via South Main Street to Route 66 motorists. He clearly believed that people would return to ballrooms and fill them as they had done before the conflict, but he could not foresee changes in musical tastes and the rise of television, which entertained people in their own homes. His ballroom operated for about a decade into the mid-1950s. Now the building is long gone.

Concurrently with Garrison's dance-hall activities, other entrepreneurs created the Holiday Inn chain of roadside motels. The first one opened in Memphis, Tennessee, in 1941, and by the mid-1950s these motels had proliferated across the United States. The enterprise eventually became one of the two largest hotel groups in the world. The corporation litigated extensively with others using the Holiday Inn name, but it appears that John R. Garrison closed his ballroom before it attracted the attention of attorneys for the motel company.

The Holiday Inn Ballroom placed an order for 12,500 composite-image postcards from Curt Teich and Company based on these two photographs. It went into production in Chicago on March 26, 1946, when printing house employees gave it stock number 6B-H1452.

HOLIDAY INN

JOPLIN
MISSOURI

Spring River Bridge, near Baxter Springs, Kansas

120807

CHAPTER THREE

KANSAS

ROUTE 66 LOOPS THROUGH THIRTEEN MILES OF KANSAS, including the towns of Galena and Baxter Springs. The first few miles pass through a zone of desolation wrought by decades of lead mining; then the way enters a verdant area of fields and scattered woods. Locals in Galena took advantage of the natural forest to create campgrounds for motorists coming from farther afield.

At one time a handsome three-span concrete Marsh arch bridge carried the travelers across the Spring River near Baxter Springs. It has disappeared, but a similar single-span bridge on old 66 has been preserved nearby over Brush Creek. Just west of the present Spring River crossing, the Old Riverton Store, established in the 1920s, at the time of writing still provided groceries, general merchandise, and cold-cut sandwiches prepared to buyers' specifications.

The scene of a raid by Civil War bandit William Quantrill, Baxter Springs in its heyday boasted a picture-perfect downtown with multiple handsome commercial buildings. There merchants supplied the needs for both locals and travelers on Highway 66 as they passed through their town headed toward either Missouri or Oklahoma.

Main Street

GALENA, KANSAS

1929

Galena, Kansas, was an industrial town. It came into existence in 1877 with discovery of lead sulfide ore, and within a month an estimated ten thousand people flooded into mining camps and surrounding areas. Eventually an estimated 25,000 people lived in the town. The place-name, Galena, comes from the scientific term for lead sulfide. From the 1870s through World War II, the Tri-State Mining District, which encompassed southeastern Kansas, northeastern Oklahoma, and southwestern Missouri, produced the majority of the lead used in the United States. As the town at the center of the district, Galena had interurban streetcars connecting with Baxter Springs, Kansas, and with Joplin and Carthage, Missouri, for transporting miners to jobs. Some of these street railway tracks are in the photograph.

From the Missouri state line at Joplin, U.S. Highway 66 passed westward for a mile and a half through an almost unearthly landscape of mines and smelters into Galena. A writer for the Federal Writers' Project guide to Kansas in 1939 observed, "Lying in all directions from the highway are man-made mountains of chert, residue from the mines, topped occasionally with gaunt black mills and separated by dusty roads, railroad tracks, and patches of rock and cinder-covered wasteland." It was along this stretch of road that Route 66 motorists in June 1935 inadvertently became involved in a brief but violent industrial action when striking miners sought to prevent nonunion workers from entering the area by stopping all traffic.

In the early 1960s Interstate 44 bypassed Galena, and during the next decade most of the lead mines were closed. The town began withering away, leaving it with about three thousand residents. Travel writer Jack D. Rittenhouse observed, "The main street has many old buildings, whose roofs are edged with the old-fashioned ornate metal cornices." This ornamentation appears in the photograph, and a number of the handsome structures remained at the time of writing, helping to make semi-depopulated Galena an interesting stop for present-day heritage tourists.

The business firm of McCarthy and Kennedy in Galena ordered one thousand "blue sky" postcards based on this photographic view northward on Main Street. The materials reached Curt Teich and Company by March 5, 1929, the date when printing staff in Chicago assigned it stock number A-953–29 and began production.

Main Street, Looking North, Galena, Kansas

953-29

Tourist Camp

GALENA, KANSAS

1929

Even though Galena was a mining town, it also offered some natural beauty, especially to the south and west, away from the immediate lead works. At least one campground for automobile tourists opened in the wooded areas as early as the 1920s.

During the pioneering days of motoring before and immediately after World War I, travelers by car typically had two choices for accommodations: they could stay overnight in a traditional downtown hotel that typically catered to traveling salesmen and railway travelers, or they could camp out beside the road. Campers carried their own gear, including tents, bedding, cooking utensils, and lanterns. Pitching one's tent along the roadside meant avoiding room rents, expenses for prepared meals, parking fees, and even tips. This economy meant that campers could go farther and see more on a limited budget.

Initially these self-sufficient vacationers squatted in likely locations, frequently not bothering to ask for permission. The trash they left behind gave rise to the derisive nickname "tin can tourists." Civic pride combined with concern for public hygiene and safety prompted municipal governments to designate specific areas for overnight auto camping. These designations allowed city authorities to police the campgrounds and prevent them from becoming resorts for less desirable, unemployed transients. The grounds usually offered central toilet facilities, picnic tables, and scattered light poles, and often cookhouses as well. The Galena Tourist Camp served this role for 1920s motorists. The photograph shows auto travelers who have set up both free-standing tents as well as canvas flies attached to the sides of their vehicles.

Stationers McCarthy and Kennedy in Galena ordered one thousand black-and-white postcards illustrating the Tourist Camp in their town. The request reached Curt Teich and Company by March 4, 1929, when staff there assigned the job stock number A-954–29 and created a production file.

5 3/16.

Tourist Camp Galena Ks.

TOURIST PARK. GALENA. KANSAS

954-29

Travelers' Inn

GALENA, KANSAS

1931

The Travelers' Inn at Galena represents a stage in the evolution of the modern roadside motel known as the cabin camp. During the early days of cross-country motoring, before and just after the First World War, many thrifty travelers eschewed staying in hotels; instead they set up and slept in their own tents or cars at the side of the road. Quickly municipal governments started designating campgrounds to regulate and care for these temporary visitors. By 1925 most municipal campgrounds charged nominal fees for space, water, tent rental, and access to bathhouses and other amenities.

As soon as entrepreneurs realized that travelers were paying for places to camp overnight, they opened competing private camps. Some travelers arrived without camping gear, and by the 1920s camp proprietors were erecting simple one-room cabins, usually in rows with spaces to park automobiles either in front or along the side. These cabin camps typically included not just huts and space for erecting tents, but also central lavatories, gasoline stations, and often lunch counters serving limited fare. During the 1930s some such cabins were expanded, becoming cottages that in time provided their own toilet, bathing, and cooking facilities; fresh linens; electrical lighting; heating; and even radios. In this way the travelers' overnight stays changed from open-air sleeping under canvas to indoor experiences inside weatherproof cabins. The photograph of the Travelers' Inn at Galena illustrates the evolution of roadside lodging into the transitional phase of cabin camps.

The Travelers' Inn auto camp ordered one thousand black-and-white postcards from Curt Teich and Company, with the request reaching the printer on October 6, 1931, the day the printing house staff assigned the job stock number IA2759.

Spring River Bridge

NEAR BAXTER SPRINGS,

KANSAS

1928

For decades motorists on U.S. Highway 66 crossed Spring River at the east side of Riverton, Kansas, on a handsome three-span reinforced concrete arch bridge. The 125-mile waterway heads in southwestern Missouri, flows through the southeastern corner of Kansas, and empties into the Grand River in northeastern Oklahoma.

During the early 1920s the Kansas Highway Commission undertook systematic efforts to improve roads in the lead-producing area around Galena and Baxter Springs to facilitate travel between the two towns. The project included creating a permanent crossing over the Spring River. To accomplish this the commission gave a contract for the construction of a distinctive reinforced-concrete arch bridge invented earlier in the century by engineer James Barney Marsh.

A native of Wisconsin, Marsh had worked for bridge design and construction firms in the Midwest since the 1880s. Having planned and erected many iron truss bridges, he set his mind to developing a bridge suited to states and counties that desired safe river crossings but had limited funds for such improvements. With these concerns in mind, he created a new form of span that combined a steel arch superstructure that was assembled on site and then encased within concrete, which added both weather protection and further strength. The structures had graceful rounded, arched "rainbow" shapes created by the concrete sheathing, which was poured in forms around the metal structures of the bowstring-style arches. The U.S. Patent Office granted Marsh a patent for the innovative concept in 1912, and he soon began marketing the economical bridges to state and county governments throughout the Midwest.

The Kansas Highway Commission chose the Marsh arch design for a three-span reinforced-concrete arch bridge to convey the Galena–Baxter Springs highway across the Spring River. Completed in 1922, the structure stood until it was removed in the 1980s following erection of a replacement. A single-span 1923–24 Marsh arch bridge across Brush Creek, the last surviving Marsh arch bridge on historic U.S. Highway 66, still stood on Southeast Fiftieth Street (an extension of North Willow Avenue) three and a half miles north of Baxter Springs at the time of writing.

The Nichols Drug Store in Baxter Springs ordered one thousand "blue sky" postcards based on this photograph of the Spring River Bridge. The paperwork reached the offices of Curt Teich and Company by June 28, 1928, the day that printers assigned the job stock number 120807 and began production.

Spring River Bridge, near Baxter Springs, Kansas

120807

Main Street

BAXTER SPRINGS, KANSAS

1928

Baxter Springs, one of the two sizable towns traversed by U.S. Highway 66 in Kansas, came into existence about 1850, when John Baxter established a frontier farm and opened a tavern near a mineral spring. The community, which had been the site of a U.S. military garrison during the Civil War, received a brief infusion of money when Texas cattle driven overland on the Shawnee Trail began arriving there in 1867. It then profited more substantially for decades from its proximity to lead deposits in the Tri-State Mining District, even becoming the terminus for an interurban railway that ran through the mineral region to Joplin and Carthage in Missouri.

The routing of U.S. 66 through Baxter Springs in 1926 brought steady trade for some of its merchants. About two years after the highway designation, a photographer stepped into the intersection of West Twelfth Street and Military Avenue, pointed his camera northward on the Mother Road along Military, and snapped the shutter to capture a scene showing busy stores, contemporary autos, and the interurban streetcar headed south.

Many of the buildings shown in the photograph remained at the time of writing. The three-story masonry structure on the left side of the intersection began as a Masonic lodge in the 1890s and then later served as a dry goods store, the Ritz motion picture theater, and a floral shop. For over two decades, from 1957 to 1980, it was known up and down Route 66 as the location of Blue Castle Restaurant, a popular destination for fried chicken dinners among motorists passing through Baxter Springs. Across the intersection the furniture store marked P. M. Clark also housed such additional enterprises as a funeral parlor and, for decades, the local J. C. Penney store.

The Nichols Drug Store in Baxter Springs ordered one thousand black-and-white postcards of the commercial district along Military Avenue in the town, asking that the location be identified on the printed card as "Main Street." The materials reached Curt Teich and Company by June 28, 1928, when publishing house staff assigned the job stock number 120806 and started the printing process. The customer must not have been satisfied with the proof of the card, however, for he provided a different street scene photograph that Teich artists subsequently retouched heavily before producing the revised card.

NORTH MAIN ST   BAXTER SPRINGS KANS

Main Street, Baxter Springs, Kansas

83

HOTEL SKIRVIN, OKLAHOMA CITY. OKLA.   105551

CHAPTER FOUR

OKLAHOMA

MANY HERITAGE TOURISTS SENSE THAT THEY HAVE REACHED the heartland of America when they cross into Oklahoma. Farms in the eastern portion and ranches in the west characterize this state, where many residents are American Indians. Some of these Native people drive cars with official license plates issued by their own tribal governments.

The landscape around Miami, near where U.S. 66 entered the state, was mostly open country with trees along its stream courses and fence rows. As motorists made their way westward in the direction of the open Great Plains, trees became fewer and shorter. The brown Oklahoma soil turned red around Luther, staying that color across the middle of the state all the way to about Sayre, where it returned to brown.

Many drivers took breaks from the road in or around Tulsa, the old Oil Capital of Oklahoma. The city boomed from petroleum production from the 1920s to the 1950s, giving it somewhat of a respite from the Great Depression. Architecture makes Tulsa a destination for lovers of the Art Deco style, which was popular during the years of the city's greatest prosperity. It was in Tulsa in the 1940s that westbound travelers likely first encountered Tex-Mex food at El Rancho Grande Restaurant, fronting directly on the Mother Road next-door to a soda pop bottling works. For those with slimmer pocketbooks, starting in 1926 the Coney Island sold hot dogs out of a modest storefront downtown, where it is still in business.

Farther down the highway travelers drove directly past the state capitol building in Oklahoma City. For decades it stood with no dome. Just north of the building travelers could pull in to one of the eateries where Beverly and Rubye Osborne in the 1930s first popularized serving fried chicken with fried potatoes, rolls, and honey but *without eating utensils*. They called the specialty Chicken in the Rough. Motorists with mechanical problems could stop in on Broadway Avenue at McDonald-Scott Chevrolet for repairs. Dozens of motels used bright neon signs to attract customers to rooms with Beauty Rest mattresses and Panel-Ray heaters.

Drivers headed west on Highway 66 through Yukon and El Reno in the direction of the open plains. Here they first entered the open fields of the wheat country, where huge cylindrical concrete "elevators" in little towns housed grain until it could be shipped out by rail on the Rock Island Line. Continuing onward, the travelers first spotted pale green sagebrush and spikey yuccas. (Farther on the latter are so common that the New Mexico legislature made yuccas their state flower.) The road continued on to tiny little Texola and just beyond it crossed over into the Lone Star State.

Sooner State Motor Kourt

MIAMI, OKLAHOMA

1952

For forty years the Sooner State Motor Kourt welcomed overnight guests traveling through Miami, Oklahoma, on U.S. 60 and U.S. 66. Mr. and Mrs. L. B. Hampton erected the nineteen-unit motel at 1405 North Main Street in 1941. They purposely located it on the west side of the street to make it easy for westbound motorists to pull right in. The couple named the new tourist court after the Sooners, non-Native settlers to the Indian Territory who illegally occupied choice claims before the formal opening of lands in 1889.

The Hamptons combined architectural styles for the U-shaped roadside complex. They used slab stone veneer, already made popular in the Ozarks of western Missouri, to sheathe their wood-frame cottages. They then added Tudor Revival–style faux half-timbering with stucco on the gable ends and green composition shingle roofing. The contrast of multihued brown stone, white stucco, and green roofs and trim must have looked appealing. Cottage interiors featured radios, tile showers and tubs, and, by the 1950s, air-conditioning and television sets. The owners planted trees and shrubs in the central courtyard, which became an inviting landscaped area. Initially an Art Deco neon sign reading "Sooner State Kourt" caught the eyes of motorists coming into Miami. Then after World War II a much more elaborate neon sign featuring a Conestoga wagon and the expanded name, "Sooner State Motor Kourt," took its place.

Multiple married couples owned and managed the Sooner State. Although Mrs. and Mrs. L. B. Hampton built the complex, they soon sold it to Mr. and Mrs. Alvin H. "Al" Echols, who ran it into the 1950s. Next came Elizabeth and Leonard Erdmann, who operated the motel for a number of years. Competition from other newer motels combined with realignment of Route 66 to the Will Rogers Turnpike in the mid-1950s forced managers of the Sooner State to limp along with decreasing numbers of customers. Structures on the commercially valuable property were razed in 1981, and at the time of writing the site was occupied by a modern bank.

Mr. and Mrs. Alvin H. Echols submitted this photograph when they ordered twelve thousand black-and-white postcards with deckled edges from Curt Teich and Company. The packet reached the printer by November 17, 1952, and company employees gave the job stock number D-10174.

5⁹/₁₆ Sqr

SOONER STATE MOTOR KOURT
Hwy. 66 and 69
MIAMI, OKLA.

Will Rogers's Birthplace

NEAR CHELSEA, OKLAHOMA

1937

One of the most popular humorists in the history of the United States was Oklahoma-born Will Rogers, who found fame first in vaudeville and later in motion pictures and radio. His birthplace about twelve miles away from U.S. Highway 66, southwest of Chelsea and north of Claremore, Oklahoma, was already a destination for sightseers before his untimely death with aviator Wiley Post in an airplane crash near Point Barrow, Alaska, in 1935.

Clement Vann Rogers, the comedian's father, in 1869 established a ranch on the Verdigris River in the Indian Territory. In 1875 he constructed a two-story log ranch house, where four years later his wife, Mary, bore a son named William Penn Adair Rogers. Both parents had partial Cherokee ancestry. It was here that Will grew to adulthood, learning the skills of a cowboy.

Will Rogers found his first big-time entertaining success as a performer of rope tricks and stand-up comedy on stage with the Ziegfeld Follies in New York City. Eventually he wrote a nationally syndicated newspaper column and starred in seventy-one motion pictures, most filmed in Hollywood. By the mid-1930s his voice reached millions of listeners each Sunday evening on the most popular weekly program broadcast on American radio, officially named *The Gulf Headliners* but known to most listeners simply as "Will Rogers's show." Over the airwaves he became beloved as a political wit who could gently poke fun at the most powerful people inside and outside government. In a typical monologue he good-naturedly declared before a nationwide audience, "I don't make jokes. I just watch the government and report the facts." Across the nation Americans mourned his early death.

In 1950 the U.S. Army Corps of Engineers began construction of a dam on the Verdigris River that in time threatened to inundate the clapboard-sided log Rogers homeplace. The family transferred ownership to the state of Oklahoma, which in 1960 relocated the home about a mile to an open hilltop overlooking the new Oologah Lake. At the time of writing, it was administered by the Will Rogers Memorial Museum of Claremore as a historic site and house museum open to the public.

The Rexall Drug Store in Chelsea, Oklahoma, requested one thousand black-and-white postcards showing Will Rogers's Birthplace in its original setting. After the printing company received the order on August 27, 1937, its artists in Chicago pasted a cut-out—a figure of Rogers from another photograph—onto the front of the ranch house picture and gave the composite postcard job their stock number 7A478.

Will Rogers' Birthplace near Chelsea, Okla.

7A478

Hotel Will Rogers

CLAREMORE, OKLAHOMA

1930

Claremore, Oklahoma, traces its beginnings to an 1802 settlement of Osage Indians and later by Cherokees in the 1850s. In 1902 an Anglo-American settler sinking a well unexpectedly punctured an aquifer containing highly mineralized water and thereby brought notoriety to the community. Smelling of "rotten eggs," these waters infused with hydrogen sulfide attracted health seekers who hoped that bathing in the "radium waters" would cure their rheumatism, intestinal problems, and skin ailments. Within a decade dozens of hotels, boardinghouses, and bathhouses sprang up to serve these visitors.

Three local businessmen, one of whom claimed to have been cured by the healing waters, in 1929 pooled their personal funds and capital from investors to erect what they envisioned as a first-class hotel to house health seekers and other travelers to Claremore. By this time U.S. Highway 66 was three years old and bringing increasing numbers of motorists through the town. The partners started construction in spring 1929. The Black Tuesday stock market crash took place on October 29 of the same year, but the promoters continued undaunted. They formally opened a handsome Spanish Renaissance Revival–style hotel with a bathhouse on the upper floor on February 7, 1930.

Although entertainer Will Rogers had no formal connection with the hotel and did not attend its dedication ceremonies, he did write about it in his national newspaper column. The native son claimed that the six-story hostelry was the "most up-to-date in the Southwest . . . [and] higher than any hotel in London." Referring to the bathhouse, he added, "It's got more baths in one room than Buckingham Palace, where the king lives."

The Will Rogers Hotel operated into the early 1990s, when it closed and the property was acquired by the Rogers County Historical Society. This organization preserves and hopes to restore and reopen portions of the notable structure.

Shortly after its 1930 dedication, the Will Rogers Hotel ordered one thousand postcards from Curt Teich and Company showing its lobby, mezzanine, and coffee shop printed in black and green ink. The materials reached the postcard publisher in Chicago by April 4, 1930, when employees assigned it stock number D-736 and initiated the printing job.

Scenes from—

HOTEL WILL ROGERS
Claremore's Newest
and Finest Hotel

Fireproof and Modern in Every Way
CLAREMORE, OKLA.

91

Ed Wright Tire Company

TULSA, OKLAHOMA

1950

Residents of Tulsa knew Ed Wright from his clever radio advertisements for automobile tires and service. Some people went so far as to call his homespun commercial announcements zany, and they must have been. The notices did encourage customers to patronize his business in a row of modest buildings at 3118 East Fifteenth Street. The location was only four blocks south of U.S. Highway 66, and his Poor Old Ed radio ads must have attracted business from drivers on the nearby Mother Road.

Wright came to Tulsa from Texas in 1935 to work for the General Tire Company. He reportedly sold so many tires in the Sooner State that he decided to stay. After serving in the army during World War II, he returned to Tulsa, where as a veteran he established the Ed Wright Tire Company about 1946. Wright installed fuel storage tanks and pumps, started selling gasoline and fixing flats, and quickly added new tires and tubes to his stock at the corner of East Fifteenth and Florence Place. Soon he built several adjoining flat-roofed masonry service bays west of his one-room Tudor Revival–style office.

Ed Wright operated his tire and auto service business at least until 1954, by which time he became involved in other enterprises. He and wife Mamie opened a dude ranch near Beggs, south of Tulsa, and they worked with a charitable organization to sponsor disadvantaged urban youths to spend time there. He also became involved in founding the Snug Harbor resort on Fort Gibson Lake, about sixty miles southeast of Tulsa, where he offered what he called "the largest fishing dock in the world." Ed Wright never claimed humility in advertising. One time he even told the press that one of his hobbies was "writing corny advertising copy."

After Wright moved on to other ventures, his successors continued to serve motorists at his former location. There they sold fuel and tires and provided repair services for over half a century. At the time of writing, the facility stood unchanged, though painted a cream color. Ed Wright himself would recognize it in a moment.

Ed Wright sent in a request for six thousand black-and-white postcards based on this photograph that he himself submitted Curt Teich and Company. The mailing reached the printer in Chicago by December 14, 1950, when it received stock number D-9728.

5⅛ Square   9 3/16

38

Beverly's Chicken in the Rough

OKLAHOMA CITY, OKLAHOMA

1951

Historians generally agree that Beverly's Chicken in the Rough was the first eatery in the United States to offer cut-up half chickens deep fried and served on beds of french fries with roll, butter, and honey but *without eating utensils.* Today people casually eat fried chicken with their fingers, but in the 1930s such behavior, at least in public, was generally considered rude and uncultured.

The story began in 1936 when Beverly (the husband) and Rubye (the wife) Osborne, owners of an Oklahoma City hamburger stand, took a road trip to California. Along the way a box of home-fried chicken bounced from the front seat onto the floor, and Rubye remarked to her husband, "This is really chicken in the rough." They picked up the pieces, brushed them off, and munched along, but the spill prompted Beverly to think about frying up chicken in their roadside stand and advising customers to eat it using their fingers. They tried it, and with a price of fifty cents for half a chicken and the trimmings and using a copyrighted cartoon of a rooster holding golf clubs, their idea of casual dining caught on. It really caught on.

The couple first added to their stand and then constructed completely new eating establishments, eventually opening eight chicken houses in Oklahoma City. The largest restaurant, pictured here, stood on Lincoln Boulevard fronting on Route 66 immediately north of the Oklahoma State Capitol. It seated a remarkable eleven hundred diners and became a favorite within walking distance of state offices for legislators and bureaucrats. One customer remembered fondly, "We state employees were paid once a month, so on payday we would sometimes go to Beverly's as a special treat." The giant chicken house operated until 1961, when its site was cleared to make way for new landscaping and traffic flow around the capitol.

Beverly and Rubye Osborne ordered 12,500 color postcards from Curt Teich and Company based on these three photographs; the artist combined them by placing portraits of the founders in the sky looking down on their eatery. The company assigned the job stock number 1C-H3 and began the production process on January 2, 1951.

Rephoto 8 3/16

(Dial 1CN3

BEVERLY OSBORNE   MRS. OSBORNE

39

Beverly and Rubye Osborne with Their Chicken in the Rough Western Girls

OKLAHOMA CITY, OKLAHOMA

1952

After Beverly and Rubye Osborne developed the idea of serving fried chicken and the trimmings to be eaten without utensils in 1936, they began opening up chicken houses throughout Oklahoma City. Eventually they operated eight restaurants in the city, but their approach to casual dining grew faster than they could manage on their own. Consequently they began one of the nation's earliest efforts at franchising restaurants: for a fee local businesspeople could open their own Chicken in the Rough restaurants. In time franchises appeared in 234 locations across the United States, a number of them along U.S. Highway 66 in places such as Amarillo, Texas, and Kingman, Arizona.

Like many other entrepreneurs, the Osbornes sought gimmicks to promote their franchises. One of these was to print colorful postcards showing their trademark rooster carrying golf clubs and use them in a contest that offered a hundred-dollar prize. The winner would be the first person each year who could eat at twenty-five of the restaurants in the chain. To prove they had been to the locations, contestants asked the store managers to sign and date the postcards before mailing them to corporate headquarters in Oklahoma City.

Another way the Osbornes attracted diners to their eight flagship restaurants was to encourage their waitstaff to dress in Hollywood-style western attire, including fancy boots. The atmosphere and good food made the eating places incredibly popular. One former high-school-age customer reminisced that any night of the week, but especially on Saturdays, he could depend on finding high school and college friends at Beverly's in Oklahoma City, plowing through hamburgers and chicken baskets. "It was more of an institution than a restaurant," he remembered. "We met there after any kind of event, from a movie to a formal dance."

Beverly and Rubye Osborne ordered 12,500 color postcards based on this photograph; Curt Teich and Company assigned it stock number 2C-P2270 on April 25, 1952. An artist in Chicago removed the top of an oil derrick and added a shade tree to give more balance to the image.

Beverly Osborne and his Chicken in the Rough Western girls going to the FFA and 4-H Club Live Stock Auction. It is the custom at Beverly's to buy a champion each year.

Garland's Drive-In Restaurant

OKLAHOMA CITY, OKLAHOMA

1942

Garland's Drive-In was both an architectural and a culinary landmark in Oklahoma City during the 1940s. With an Art Deco spire soaring above its dining room, the restaurant occupied prime real estate just south of the intersection of busy north–south Broadway Avenue with east–west Northwest Twenty-Third Street, which carried both Route 66 and local traffic from the Oklahoma state capitol building to the city's western precincts.

Garland B. Arrington, who earlier had worked in the state capitol cafeteria, opened his drive-in restaurant in 1939. Customers could eat inside or park outside for curb service. They enjoyed such specialties of the house as Tennessee-style country ham, fried chicken, and individual chicken pot pies. Garland's became a popular meeting place for ladies' luncheons, wedding rehearsal dinners, and other social gatherings. On weekends during the 1940s it became the haunt of local teenagers, who drove their cars back and forth along four-lane Broadway between the central business district and fashionable Twenty-Third Street.

Arrington's classified advertisements in the *Oklahoman* newspaper shed some light on what it was like to work at Garland's Drive-In. In January 1943, for example, he solicited applications for employment of a "first-class fry cook," adding that they "must be fast." A month later he posted this notice: "Wanted waitress, full or part time, good salary and tips." Two years later, reflecting the segregated Oklahoma City society, he advertised that he was seeking an "exp[erienced] Colored salad woman."

In 1947 Arrington sold Garland's Drive-In, but it never thrived so well as it had under his management. Its site today is obliterated by modern construction in the vicinity of the Winnans Park Fire Station Number 5. Garland himself went on to operate the successful Boulevard Cafeteria on Classen Boulevard during the 1950s.

In late 1942 Garland's Drive-In Restaurant requested sixty-five hundred color postcards from Curt Teich and Company based on this nighttime photograph. The printing order went into production in Chicago just before Christmas, on December 23, 1942.

El Fenix Restaurant

OKLAHOMA CITY, OKLAHOMA

1950

After Luis Alvarado and his Cuellar family in-laws from Texas introduced Tex-Mex cooking to Oklahoma City diners at El Charro Café about 1939, other enterprising businesspeople took notice. Not only did occasional grassroots competitors spring up, but rivals also came onto the scene with substantial experience in the business. One of these very capable new entrants to the Mexican food scene in Oklahoma was Gilbert Martinez, from the venerable El Fenix Restaurants in Dallas.

Miguel "Mike" Martinez, Gilbert's father, opened his first café serving American-style dishes in Dallas in 1918 and later added Mexican fare. In 1922 he expanded the eatery, renaming it El Fenix after the mythical phoenix, reborn from the ashes of its predecessor. Today Martinez is known for the innovation of offering Mexican food combination plates identified by number so English-speaking customers would not have to stumble over Spanish-language words while placing orders.

About 1950 son Gilbert Martinez moved to Oklahoma City. That year he opened a brand-new El Fenix Restaurant at the intersection of North Broadway Boulevard and Northwest Twenty-Second Street, the same address as the once popular Garland's Drive-In Restaurant, just one block south of east–west Route 66 across the city along Northwest Twenty-Third Street. The new building incorporated elements of the fashionable International architectural style, and it included a two-story-tall circular neon sign bearing the words "EL FENIX RESTAURANT."

As the person who a decade before had helped familiarize Oklahoma City diners with Mexican cooking, Luis Alvarado at El Charrito might have resented the Martinez family from Dallas for intruding into his business territory. Little could he have predicted that competition on North Broadway would be short-lived. By 1955 El Fenix had closed, and the next year Luis Alvarado opened his own El Charrito Café Number Three in the very same building.

El Fenix Restaurant in Oklahoma City requested 12,500 composite-view color postcards from Curt Teich and Company based on these photographs, and the job received stock number 0C-H1322 on August 3, 1950. On the card Teich artists reproduced the drawing of a Mexican dancer from the front of a menu provided by the customer.

Rephoto 3

Rephoto 3½   OCN 1322

Rephoto 8¼   OCN 1322

2300 N. BROADWAY
OKLAHOMA CITY, OKLA.

AMERICAN
AND
SEA FOOD DISHES

McDonald-Scott Chevrolet Company

OKLAHOMA CITY, OKLAHOMA

1944

North Broadway Avenue just north of downtown Oklahoma City from the 1920s to 1940s was its "automobile alley." The thoroughfare was the widest north–south street in Oklahoma City when the town was laid out in 1889, and by the time automobiles came along in the early twentieth century, this breadth made the avenue an ideal location for car dealerships. North Broadway between Northwest Fourth and Northwest Twelfth eventually was lined with motor vehicle dealers, auto accessory stores, body shops, garages, and service stations. Most of these historic buildings survive today, and the district is filled with popular eateries, clubs, and retail outlets.

McDonald Chevrolet Company was one of the prominent enterprises in the historic North Broadway "automobile alley." The enterprise had its beginning with Robert P. McDonald about 1935, when his Chevrolet dealership occupied a storefront at 825 North Broadway. About 1937 he erected a new building at the south end of the same block, at number 801. It had a spacious new-car showroom with big display windows fronting on North Broadway; an even larger service department in the rear had overhead doors opening onto Northwest Seventh. Before long the enterprise extended northward into an adjoining older commercial building at 807.

About 1942 R. Thornton Scott joined Robert P. McDonald in what came to be known as McDonald-Scott Chevrolet. For years the two men ran the business together, and then Scott bought the whole business. As Scott Chevrolet Company the dealership remained on North Broadway long after most of its competitors had relocated to the suburbs. Finally Scott Chevrolet made the move as well. Today the buildings remain much as they appear in these 1940s photographs; an automotive body and paint shop occupies the corner at 801 North Broadway, and there is a specialty retail outlet in the 1920s commercial building at 807. Exterior painting on the upper housing for a freight elevator in the old building complex still reads "Scott Chevrolet."

McDonald-Scott Chevrolet Company ordered 12,500 color postcards from Curt Teich and Company based on these two photographs. The printer began production on January 25, 1944, giving the job stock number 3B-H1260. The reverse side was imprinted in dark blue with an advertisement encouraging automobile owners to bring their cars in for regular service. In light of shortages on the home front during World War II, the dealer advised, "Treat your car right and it will last you 'for the duration.'"

STRIGHTEN

Straighten 8"

Right 6

3184 1260

McDONALD-SCOTT

CHEVROLET
COMPANY

OKLAHOMA CITY
OKLAHOMA

El Charro Café

OKLAHOMA CITY, OKLAHOMA

1942

When he wed Mary Cuellar in 1932, Mexican-born Luis Alvarado married into a clan that would become famous for its food. His mother-in-law, Adelaide Cuellar, was the matriarch of the family that in the 1940s started a chain of Tex-Mex restaurants called El Chico, which remain popular today in seven states of the Sun Belt.

Luis Alvarado had worked in commercial kitchens in San Antonio and Dallas when he and two brothers-in-law, Gilbert and Macario Cuellar, moved to Oklahoma City sometime around 1937. By 1939 they had secured backers to open a Mexican café in an Art Deco commercial building at the northeast corner of the intersection of Northwest Tenth Street and North Dewey Avenue in downtown. They called it El Charro, "The Cowboy."

This was no hole-in-the-wall chili parlor. Instead it was an appealing sit-down restaurant with imposing murals and strolling musicians. On the menu, however, were the time-tested dishes created by Adelaide Cuellar. Specialties included guacamole salad, chicken tacos, and huevos rancheros. Once Luis and wife Mary became firmly situated running their café in Oklahoma City, Gilbert and Mack Cuellar returned to Texas. There in 1940 in the Oak Lawn district of Dallas, they and other Cuellar brothers opened another eatery similarly called El Charro, but they soon changed its name to El Chico, meaning "The Little Boy" or "The Rascal." It was the birthplace of the El Chico restaurant chain.

In the meantime Luis and Mary Cuellar Alvarado continued to operate their downtown Oklahoma City El Charro until 1947. The previous year they had opened a new eatery, El Charrito, "The Little Cowboy," at 2909 Paseo, and it and others succeeded so well that in time they had six restaurants. As Luis approached retirement age in 1967, he sold his Oklahoma eating places to his Texas relatives, who converted them to part of the El Chico chain. The old, original downtown El Charro building, which has long been used for other purposes, at the time of writing still stood on the northeast corner of Tenth and Dewey. Its diagonal corner entry and windows now covered with masonry, the structure housed part of the headquarters for the Emergency Medical Services Authority in Oklahoma City.

El Charro Café ordered 12,500 composite color postcards from Curt Teich and Company based on these photographs. The materials reached the printer in Chicago by June 1, 1942, when Teich employees assigned the job stock number 2B-H558 and began production.

Skirvin Hotel

OKLAHOMA CITY, OKLAHOMA

1925

For decades the Skirvin offered travelers some of the finest hotel rooms in Oklahoma City, and it still does, thanks to its 2007 renovation. The story of the venerable hostelry goes back to 1909, when a New York investor tried to buy four downtown lots from oilman William B. Skirvin and inadvertently mentioned that he wanted to use them to build "the biggest hotel" in the new state of Oklahoma. Put off by the outsider's boast, the successful local businessman decided to construct the lodgings himself.

Working with architect Solomon A. Layton, Skirvin projected a U-shaped hotel consisting of two south-facing towers connected by a rounded bay. As construction progressed, the height was increased from six to ten stories, delaying opening of the 225-room hotel until September 1911. The oilman succeeded in his efforts to create the finest hotel in the city. Any out-of-town visitor who "was anybody" typically stayed there. During the Roaring Twenties oil boom followed oil boom in the Sooner State, and Bill Skirvin and downtown Oklahoma City both prospered. Good fortune prompted Skirvin to add a third south-facing tower in 1923, giving the hotel the appearance it has in this photograph.

In early 1928 it seemed that economic prosperity would last forever. Bill Skirvin had architect Solomon Layton draw up plans to build all three towers up to fourteen stories while refurbishing the whole building. The project, completed in April 1930, included a popular roof garden, ballroom, and restaurant on the upper level. In this basic configuration the Skirvin Hotel operated through the middle years of the twentieth century. After William Skirvin's death in 1944, ownership passed through multiple hands until 1988, when the hotel closed, a victim of downtown decline and changing tastes in lodging. Nineteen years later a public-private partnership raised over $50 million for renovation, and the hotel reopened in 2007 as the Skirvin Hilton. The hotel again offers travelers what many consider the best rooms in Oklahoma City.

J. Thomas McHaney, manager of the National Studio in Oklahoma City, requested ten thousand color postcards based on this photograph from Curt Teich and Company. The Chicago printing house gave the job stock number A-105531 and started production on August 17, 1925.

HOTEL SKIRVIN, OKLAHOMA CITY, OKLA. 105551

Venetian Room, Skirvin Hotel

1936

When William B. Skirvin expanded his Skirvin Hotel in downtown Oklahoma City to fourteen stories tall in 1928–30, he placed a large ballroom atop the westernmost of the three connecting towers. Because the large open space was decorated in the style of the Italian Renaissance, he called it the Venetian Room. Decorators covered the walls with tapestries and murals depicting scenes in Venice and lighted it with Venetian-style lanterns and three large chandeliers. Architect Solomon A. Layton designed the floor specifically for dancing, in red and white oak squares in a parquet pattern polished to a high sheen.

Although the Great Depression had begun with the stock market crash on October 29, 1929, Oklahoma City for a time seemed immune to its economic effects. The newly developed Oklahoma City oil field, which brought derricks right into the city proper, fueled the economy of the state capital, delaying effects of the national economic crisis. Free-flowing money enabled Bill Skirvin to feature a different big-city dance band each month to entertain guests at the Venetian Room dinner club. During its first two years it showcased fifteen different dance bands, twelve of which were considered "big name" orchestras.

On the day when the photograph was taken, Bernie Cummins and his New Yorker Hotel Orchestra had set up to play for dancers in the Venetian Room. Bernard Joseph "Bernie" Cummins had organized his first dance band in 1919, and it grew into a nationally known orchestra that in the 1920s and 1930s made multiple commercial recordings. The group not only performed at the New Yorker Hotel and other New York venues and at multiple hotels in Chicago, but also participated in a regular circuit through the Midwest, including Oklahoma City. Despite the growing popularity of other dance forms, the orchestra stayed together until 1959.

When the Skirvin was renovated between 2005 and 2007, the Venetian Room was returned to its former glory. At the time of writing, it was serving as a large ballroom space in the Skirvin Hilton.

The Skirvin Hotel placed an order for 12,500 color postcards based on this photograph. It went into production on January 8, 1936, when the job received stock number 6A-H69.

THE VENETIAN ROOM — SKIRVIN HOTEL — OKLAHOMA CITY, OKLA.   6A-H69

46

Herman's Restaurant

OKLAHOMA CITY, OKLAHOMA

1951

Herman O. Baggett prepared food almost his entire life. Learning to cook for others in the army during World War I, the Texan relocated to Oklahoma City in 1925 and pursued food service. He first worked at Bishop's Waffle House until 1936, when with Alex S. Weiss he opened Herman's Grill at 110 West First Street, an upscale downtown location across from the WKY radio studios in the Skirvin Tower.

By 1939 Baggett moved his business to 500 North Hudson Avenue in downtown and renamed it Herman's Sea Food Restaurant. According to his daughter, "Daddy was bringing in fresh seafood when that sort of thing was unheard of. It came packed in ice every day." This type of food was exceptional during the hard times at the end of the Great Depression, but people who had money in their pocketbooks from the Oklahoma City oil field could afford such luxuries. Well-heeled travelers on Route 66 could drop down to Herman's to indulge their tastes in fresh fish even though they were five hundred miles from the nearest coast.

Baggett's restaurant survived multiple fires and burglaries on Hudson Avenue before it moved in 1950 to a much larger purpose-built facility at the upper end of a gently sloping parking lot at the busy three-way intersection of Classen Boulevard, Northwest Sixteenth Street, and North Western Avenue. This placed it just six blocks south of U.S. Highway 66 along Northwest Twenty-Third Street. Atop the building a giant neon sign featuring a fish jumping out of water beckoned to motorists. Inside the kitchen Herman supervised food preparation, while his wife, Mary May Baggett, ran the dining room. Their successful collaboration made Herman's Sea Food an Oklahoma City institution. The couple ran the fish house until 1968, by which time the local press was calling it "the oldest seafood eating place in the state." After its sale to a local food service company, the enterprise operated under the Herman's name another decade. Since then a number of other restaurants have come and gone inside the historic building, which at the time of writing still stood at 1011 Northwest Sixteenth Street.

Herman's Restaurant itself requested 12,500 composite color postcards from Curt Teich and Company based in part on these photographs. The job went into production in Chicago with stock number D-9920 on November 7, 1951.

47

Patrick's Drive-In Food

OKLAHOMA CITY, OKLAHOMA

1951

In American English the term "drive-in" refers either to a nighttime open-air venue for viewing motion pictures from parked automobiles or to an eating place serving food delivered directly to motorists' parked cars. Patrick's Drive-In fronting on Route 66 at 1016 Northwest Twenty-Third Street in Oklahoma City began its operation as the latter category of enterprise.

Patrick and Mary A. Williams opened Patrick's Drive-In Food about 1951, the same year that they ordered sixty-five hundred color postcards from Curt Teich and Company. The eating place stood at the prime southeast corner of the intersection of Northwest Twenty-Third Street (Route 66) with North Western Avenue, about six blocks north of Herman's Restaurant. Initially the restaurant offered curb service, as denoted by its "drive-in" name. It featured quickly prepared fried foods like hamburgers and french fries combined with soda-fountain service of ice cream, flavored syrups, and carbonated beverages. Quickly Patrick's became more than just a popular pull-in streetside eatery. With upholstered booths and a jukebox, its customers became regulars and began scheduling celebratory functions like wedding showers in the conveniently located restaurant.

About 1963 Mary and Patrick Williams sold the drive-in to established restaurateur E. Clinton "Sandy" Sanders. He and his wife, Ruth, operated eating places in Cordell, Oklahoma, before moving to Oklahoma City in 1948. Continuing in the food service business in the city, Sanders undoubtedly admired the strategic street-junction location of Patrick's Drive-In Food. About 1963 "Sandy" Sanders had an opportunity to purchase Patrick's and chose to operate the eatery under its original name. The businessman was about to enter a new late-in-life career, having been elected to the Oklahoma Legislature in 1970. Reelected multiple times, he served until 1986. In the meantime, about 1975, Sanders sold Patrick's Drive-In. At the time of writing, the site was occupied by a convenience store that benefited from the traffic flow at the same busy intersection that attracted Patrick Williams in 1951.

Shortly after it opened, Patrick's Drive-In ordered sixty-five hundred composite-image color postcards based in part on this photograph featuring its neon sign. Curt Teich and Company gave the printing job stock number 1C-H703 and began work on the card on May 24, 1951.

Just a little
DIFFERENT — — *twenty third & northwestern — Oklahoma City*

Phillips Courts

EL RENO, OKLAHOMA

1954

For three-quarters of a century the Phillips Courts have provided lodging for travelers at El Reno, the first county-seat town west of Oklahoma City on U.S. Highway 66. The community had its origins in an 1870s U.S. Army garrison at Fort Reno, just to the west, and it grew into a substantial town from harvests of wheat raised on the surrounding open plains.

During the 1920s many motorists who did not stay overnight in traditional town-center hotels chose instead to camp beside their cars. Some did so in the country, while others bedded down in community-run and privately operated auto campgrounds. By 1938 Samuel Falk operated one of these camps and an adjacent filling station next to the bulk petroleum depot of the Phillips Petroleum Company. The location on the west side of El Reno fronted on U.S. Highway 66 at 1221 Sunset Drive.

By 1941 management of the campground with cabins had shifted to John R. and Ola Phillips. Together they operated the lodging place, and he also served as the agent for the Phillips bulk oil facility. In time the couple expanded the courts into a capital E "footprint," with five rows of connected cabins under long gabled roofs. During the 1960s they sold the property to Kneeles M. and Louise Reeves, who added a café facing the street and ran both for years. The motel changed hands a few more times, and in the 1990s it became the Budget Inn, under which name it continued offering overnight accommodations at the time of writing.

The Phillips Courts ordered twenty-five thousand extra-length double color postcards from Curt Teich and Company, which on July 28, 1954, gave the job stock number D-10596. John and Ola Phillips provided a series of side-by-side pictures showing the full length of the tourist court, as well as a separate photograph of the neon sign in front of the office. Herbert Burns, who assisted with the order, on July 17, 1954, wrote, "Mrs. Phillips wants this sign placed . . . with the angle changed so that the lettering will be readable."

Phone 251 — 1221 Sunset Drive — El Reno, Oklahoma

THE PLACE TO STAY — WHEN IN AMARILLO, TEXAS!

BUNGALOW COURTS — 1004 NORTH FILLMORE — On U. S. Highway 87, and convenient to 60 and 66

CHAPTER FIVE

TEXAS

EVERY STATE TRIES TO PRESENT A GOOD IMPRESSION, and this is what Texas and Oklahoma did at their shared state line. U.S. Highway 66 in both Oklahoma and Texas was mostly a narrow, two-lane roadway except in a few towns. When it approached the state line, however, the pavement widened into two paved lanes in each direction, with a grassy median in the center. The imposing stretch of concrete lasted for only about half a mile, but officials in both states must have prided themselves in constructing a roadway that would demonstrate how progressive they were, if only for a short distance.

Out-of-state drivers must have been unimpressed once they got into Texas. Initially they observed long vistas along gullies reminiscent of western movie landscapes, but after about fifty miles the road climbed onto the table-top-flat plains. The scattered trees were all oddly shaped by the prevailing winds and looked like they were leaning toward the northeast. Once drivers reached the flat plains, trees effectively disappeared except where humans had planted them, and the natural vegetation became short grass. There was not very much to see other than the narrow two lanes of pavement that led in the direction of the setting sun. During dust storms of the 1930s, windblown sand became so abrasive that it blasted painted finishes on the fronts of cars down to bare metal. Wintertime blizzards could completely shut down the thoroughfare for days at a time, stranding motorists in little places like Shamrock and Conway.

Other than occasional county-seat towns, the only real city drivers traversed in Texas was Amarillo, which thrived from wheat, cattle, strategic railway lines, and cross-country motorists. Its east and west sides boasted rows of tourist courts, filling stations, and eating places. Lodgings like the Bungalow Court and the Sunset Motel catered to transients, giving them shelter for the night. Many people remembered stays in Amarillo due to mechanical breakdowns and complained about the high prices they were charged for repairs. "Let me tell you about the time my generator went out in Amarillo . . . ," they would recount with distaste. Others, by contrast, would praise the deep-sea fish they enjoyed at the Longchamp Dining Salon, seven hundred miles from the ocean. As early as the 1940s owner Homer Rice was flying in seafood six days a week for freshness.

Westward from Amarillo the flat landscape grew even drier. Places to stop for fuel, repairs, refreshments, and accommodation became more widely scattered. At Adrian travelers reached the midpoint between Chicago and Los Angeles, but many must have thought they had reached the ends of the earth. Onward they pushed to Glenrio, a wide spot in the road divided into two, one-half on each side of the Texas–New Mexico state line. There Homer Ehresman for years was pleased to sell them expensive gasoline at his combined filling station, café, and motel.

Oldham's State Line Station

EAST OF SHAMROCK, TEXAS

1952

Oldham's State Line Station was a gasoline filling station that operated on U.S. Highway 66 about thirteen miles east of Shamrock, Texas, just west of the Texas boundary with Oklahoma. The Texas and Oklahoma highway departments expanded about half a mile of pavement straddling the state line into four lanes, two on each side of a grassy median. Oldham's station, which predated the enhancement, stood in this middle space. This position inspired the clever owner to install gasoline pumps on both sides so that he could sell fuel conveniently to both east- and westbound drivers. Later the highway departments further improved the roadway and removed the station completely.

Texaco seemed to be an appropriate brand of gasoline for westbound Route 66 motorists to encounter when they first crossed into the Lone Star State, since its name had been shortened from the Texas Company. The firm came into existence in 1902 at Beaumont, Texas, in the wake of the discovery of the great Spindletop Oil Field the year before. In 1909 the firm registered its first trademark, a large red star with a green letter *T* superimposed. The version of the logo shown in the photograph was developed in the late 1930s by designer Walter Dorwin Teague.

Some filling station owners enjoyed displaying their own personalities in their business enterprises, and Oldham's was no different. Each side of the building bore a painted list of the driving distances to destinations east or west on Route 66. The eastbound side shown in the picture listed nearby places like Erick and Sayre, Oklahoma, along with St. Louis and Chicago, but added China with question marks at the bottom.

Oldham's State Line Station ordered 12,500 color business cards based on this photograph. After the materials arrived in Chicago, on October 7, 1952, Curt Teich and Company assigned it stock number 2C-H1230, its artists retouched the image heavily, and staff members calculated distances east and west for a mileage table that was printed on the reverse side.

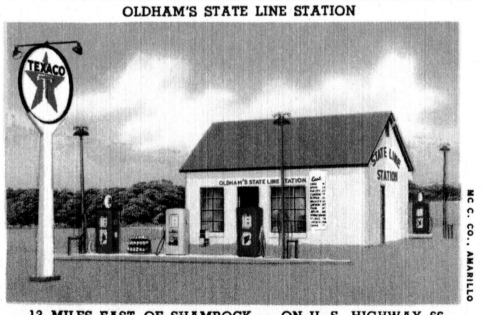

OLDHAM'S STATE LINE STATION

13 MILES EAST OF SHAMROCK — ON U. S. HIGHWAY 66

Shamrock Court

SHAMROCK, TEXAS

1952

Starting in the 1940s, the Shamrock Court offered overnight accommodations to travelers passing through Shamrock, the first town encountered by westbound Route 66 motorists after crossing from Oklahoma into Texas. Here east–west U.S. 66 intercepted north–south U.S. 83. The juncture was marked in 1934 by construction of a concrete Art Deco fantasy, the combined Tower Station and U Drop In Restaurant, which became an architectural and culinary landmark. Five blocks west of the regionally known eating place, Cleve Hamilton for years operated the Shamrock Court.

Like many contemporary motels, the Shamrock Court consisted of a series of cabins that shared long gable roofs with space for motorists to park under the shelter between the units. The motel began with a U-shaped plan built around a two-story manager's office and residence. Later another L-shaped addition was built just to the east. As early as 1949 travel writer Duncan Hines began listing the Shamrock Court in his annual guide to roadside lodging, commenting that its twenty-eight rooms were available year-round and offered such comforts as air-conditioning in the summer and panel ray heating in the winter. The enterprise operated profitably for decades but at the time of writing stood abandoned on the south side of former U.S. Highway 66 at the west edge of town.

When the locality received its first post office in 1890, Irish-born postmaster George Nickel named the town Shamrock. Since that time the community has been known for its Irish identity. Each year since 1938 residents and out-of-town visitors have celebrated an Irish festival on the weekend nearest to March 17, St. Patrick's Day. The event features a beauty pageant, beard-growing competitions, country music performances, and riding lawnmower races.

Cleve Hamilton ordered 12,500 color postcards of his Shamrock Court during late summer 1952. The request reached Curt Teich and Company in Chicago by August 7, when printing house employees gave the job stock number 2CH-1002 and started the production process.

Shamrock Court, Shamrock, Texas

51

Pueblo Court

AMARILLO, TEXAS

1935

The Pueblo Court, originally Pueblo Cibola Court, exemplified an architectural style that developed in the American Southwest during the 1920s. Architect Mary Jane Colter played an instrumental role in its development by designing commercial buildings in the region for restaurateur and hotelier Fred Harvey. As early as 1905 she began modeling her designs on the buildings of the indigenous Pueblo Indians, and by the 1920s she and others combined the mostly cubist Native American forms with increasingly fashionable geometric and ethnic ornamentation popularized in Europe by creators of the Art Deco style. The fusion came to be known as Pueblo Deco. The popularity of this distinctive southwestern style moved eastward from New Mexico to Texas and beyond, finding vernacular expression in multiple tourist courts erected at various points along U.S. Highway 66. The mid-1930s Pueblo Court in Amarillo exemplified the style, as did some of the design elements in the roughly contemporary 1931 Potter County Courthouse, which also fronted on Route 66 in the Texas Panhandle city.

The Pueblo Court included many of the features typifying Pueblo Deco architecture. Its stucco-covered, mostly rectangular buildings had somewhat rounded corners and irregularly shaped parapets. Distinctive flat roofs gave the appearance of being supported on horizontal log beams, while the tops of square-headed windows were supported on simulated timber lintels. The exterior treatment had a basic earthen color, simulating mud plaster used by the Puebloan peoples.

The Pueblo Court at 3101 Northeast Eighth Avenue (later Amarillo Boulevard East) was one of the first motels that Route 66 motorists encountered as they entered the city from the east. For some it probably represented the first example of Pueblo Deco that they had seen, and as such it must have made a strong impression. The lodging remained in business into the mid-1950s.

The management of the Pueblo Court ordered sixty-five hundred color postcards based on this photograph from Curt Teich and Company, which assigned the job stock number 5A-H1832 on October 11, 1935. Instructions called for the company artists to eliminate overhead electrical wires and add several green shrubs in front of the office at the end of the drive.

Pueblo Cíbola

● One of the entrance arches to Pueblo Cibola at Amarillo, Texas, known as the finest tourist court in the Southwest. Located at the east city limits on U. S. Highways 60 and 66, and surrounded by beautifully landscaped grounds. Pueblo Cibola combines ultra-modern accommodations with the charm of early Pueblo Indian architecture and furnishings.

52

Pueblo Court and Station

AMARILLO, TEXAS

1940

Beginning in the mid-1930s as a U-shaped stucco tourist court enclosing a landscaped courtyard, the Pueblo Court by 1940 expanded to include a filling station and additional free-standing motel units that formed a complex built in the Pueblo Deco architectural style. All the buildings had rectangular shapes, rounded corners, and flat roofs with simulated horizontal timber beams reminiscent of the Pueblo Indian dwellings in the Desert Southwest. Unlike many of its competitors along Route 66, the Pueblo Court sat back about 150 feet from the roadway, giving it a quieter atmosphere.

For years J. Wilkie Talbert operated the court and its adjacent Texaco and later Standard gasoline filling station on the east side of Amarillo. When the American Automobile Association was preparing its *Western Tour Book* for 1940, Talbert paid extra for it to include a careful description of his place of business. The guide described the court as consisting of "20 delightful apartments of Southwestern Indian architecture, each with private tile shower, toilet and lavatory" and having "beautiful handmade furniture of Indian design." Two years before, in 1938, Duncan Hines also commented on the handsome room interiors with "California Monterey furniture, Indian design." In 1942 Hines observed further, "Wilkie Talbert is as hospitable a host as you will meet on your trip."

About 1945 a changing series of new managers took over the tourist court and filling station, as the Pueblo Court began showing its age. By the early 1950s the old tourist court was beginning to suffer competition from more modern motels that offered swimming pools and coffee shops. In 1954 the Amarillo city directory showed no listing for the filling station, and in 1955 the Flamingo Motel took the place of the Pueblo Court at 3101 Northeast Eighth Street (now Amarillo Boulevard East). Owners of the newer hostelry covered some of the older buildings with a brick veneer and added on to them, almost completely obscuring the Pueblo Deco architecture that had made the Pueblo Court so distinctive. At the time of writing, even the Flamingo Motel was gone; an automobile car wash stood in its place, and no traces of the old-time roadside lodging were visible.

J. Wilkie Talbert enclosed these photographs when he requested twenty-five thousand color postcards from Curt Teich and Company, which on December 10, 1940, gave the printing job stock number 0B-H2608.

Rock-Wool Insulated against Heat and Cold

ON U. S. 66 and 60 at EAST CITY LIMITS, AMARILLO, TEXAS
— Authorized Standard Oil Lubrication —

Smith's Motel

AMARILLO, TEXAS

1945

Smith's Motel occupied an unconventional, L-shaped piece of ground close to the most important highway junction in Amarillo. This was where North Fillmore Street crossed Northeast Eighth Avenue (later Amarillo Boulevard East). Here the main east–west highways, U.S. 60 and 66, came together with the principal north–south roadways, U.S. 87 and 287.

Someone else had purchased and already occupied the small business lots at the actual northeast corner of the intersection, but entrepreneur H. Ernest Smith acquired the property immediately behind the corner lot to the north and east. About 1938–39 he skillfully constructed a tourist court that economically used the space available to create as many rooms as possible while at the same time providing direct access to both North Fillmore and Northeast Eighth. He built motel units right up to the sidewalk, created ample vehicular entrances, and erected large lighted signs inviting travelers to park their cars and spend the night in comfort.

Smith's Motel consisted of one L-shaped unit with wings both east–west and north–south plus an additional I-shaped block of rooms running east–west. Carports, built integrally with the rest of the court, provided roomside covered parking for automobiles. Smith constructed the flat-roofed buildings from ceramic tile blocks covered with white-painted stucco. Their simplicity of design showed the influence of the popular Streamline Moderne architectural style. Among the few ornaments were cornices on the exterior walls that handsomely stepped back in two courses.

Smith's Motel served travelers for almost twenty years, all of that time under the management of H. Ernest Smith and his wife, Annie. The tourist court was not his only business interest, for all of this time he also was associated with the S & M Drug Company of Amarillo, and he remained in that trade after the motel closed about 1957. Today all of the old tourist court is gone except for a small section that fronts at 307 East Amarillo Boulevard. At the time of writing, this last remaining rump from the old motel complex housed a barbershop.

Smith's Motel placed an order for 12,500 color postcards from Curt Teich and Company based on these photographs. The printing house received the materials by August 3, 1945, and gave the job stock number 5B-H766.

U. S. Highways 60 and 66, Entrance to SMITH'S MOTEL, Amarillo, Texas, 307 N. E. Eighth (Panhandle Highway)

MC C., CO. PHOTOS 53548

5B-H766

U. S. Highways 87 and 287, Entrance to SMITH'S MOTEL, Amarillo, Texas, 806 N. Fillmore St.

54

Longchamp Dining Salon

AMARILLO, TEXAS

1949

F. Homer Rice knew how to make money, and he was good at it. For several years in the 1940s he operated a Phillips 66 gasoline station and sold used cars just north of the most important highway intersection in Amarillo, Texas—the intersection of U.S. Highways 60 and 66 east–west with U.S. 87 and 287 north–south. After watching all the traffic that passed by the juncture, he concluded in 1946 that there was more money to be made feeding motorists than in selling them fuel.

The businessman knew that location was a key element of success in serving travelers. Consequently he watched when Harry G. Kindig in 1945 opened an eating place called the Longchamp Café at 705 Northeast Eighth Avenue (later Amarillo Boulevard East), just four blocks east of the major highway junction where Rice ran his filling station. In 1947 Rice purchased the café business and converted it into a high-class eatery he called the Longchamp Dining Salon. It operated in a sleek, cream-colored brick building with a fashionable round porthole window in the front. There Rice specialized in seafood, so his initial neon sign on steel poles above the roof bore a stylized swordfish. The Longchamp was the first restaurant in Amarillo to fly in fresh fish, advertising widely, "If it swims, we have it." The impressive menu included Maine lobster, Florida pompano, Gulf shrimp, red snapper, flounder, and Colorado trout, in addition to steak and chicken dinners for non-fish-eaters. In 1948 a customer named Mabel sent a Longchamp postcard home to New York State, reporting, "Had dinner here tonight. It's a lovely place."

It appears that some customers may have mistakenly associated the Longchamp with seafood only, for about 1953 the restaurant became Rice's Dining Salon. Nothing major changed in the management, and the menu still featured fresh fish along with other dishes. The owner replaced the old neon swordfish with a larger sign mounted directly on the roof reading "Rice's Dining Salon." With good food, courteous service, convenient parking, and three separate dining rooms, the place boomed. About 1962 Rice added an adjacent motel, Rice's Motor Hotel, bringing in additional diners and adding income from overnight lodgers. Then in 1968 Interstate 40 opened, diverting most east–west traffic away from old Route 66. Business declined and F. Homer Rice was aging, so he brought in outside managers to handle the waning trade at his restaurant and motel. Eventually he retired, and the two business places limped along for a few more years, into the 1980s, before they closed. Today no visible evidence remains at the site.

The McCormick advertising agency in Amarillo, Texas, ordered 25,000 composite color postcards of the Longchamp Dining Salon from Curt Teich and Company based on these photographs. The Chicago-based printing house received the materials and gave the job stock number 9B-H686 on June 7, 1949.

Bungalow Courts

AMARILLO, TEXAS

1936

For a quarter century travelers through Amarillo, Texas, found shelter for the night at the Bungalow Courts at 1004 North Fillmore Street, just two blocks north of the U.S. 60 and 66 intersection with U.S. 87 and 287. The motel did not start in this location, however. As early as 1927 John P. Schroeder operated "Bungalow Court" cabins, first at 1001 North Pierce Street and then, by 1928, at 311 East North Tenth Avenue. He and wife Marie maintained the latter location until 1932, when they opened the hostelry at its final location on North Fillmore. Within a few months John died, but his widow continued running the tourist court for years in conjunction with partners Albert N. and Bernice Washburn.

The Bungalow Courts consisted of two rows of wood-frame cabins. Each one was separated from the other by a covered garage fitted with hinged doors. The two detached wings had long gable roofs. Rooms opened onto a landscaped yard with a white picket fence and ornamental plantings. Travel writer Duncan Hines in 1938 noted that the Amarillo motel had thirty two- to four-room apartments, all with showers or tubs, while a 1939 directory issued by a local newspaper reported the lodging offered its guests "Simmons beds and Beauty Rest mattresses." Mrs. Schroeder and her partners advertised in 1939 that the Bungalow Courts were "not the newest, but the best" in the city.

About 1947 Forrest W. Ansley assumed the management of the Bungalow Courts. Later he was joined by Price Hooks and J. Lee Sparks, the two men who operated the motel until its closure about 1959. A guest at the Bungalow Courts in 1955 sent one of its postcards to a family member in Port Arthur, Texas, reporting, "Spent the night here Wed. . . . When the lady gave me the card, she said if you like it, you can stop and spend the night when you come."

The Bungalow Courts ordered six thousand color postcards based on this photograph during the hot summer of 1936. Curt Teich and Company received the materials by August 5, 1936, assigning the job stock number 6A-H1591. A note enclosed with the order asked for the artists to render the view appealing to potential guests: "Get away from the suggestion . . . of the Bungalow Courts being out . . . with nothing but flat prairie back of it. . . . You might show some Lombardy Poplars . . . over the red roof . . . and get away from the thought that the surroundings of the property are rather barren." As the printed card shows, the artists did add two nonexistent rows of trees behind the cabins.

THE PLACE TO STAY — WHEN IN AMARILLO, TEXAS!

MCC CO. 4302-H

6A-H1591

BUNGALOW COURTS — 1004 NORTH FILLMORE — On U. S. Highway 87, and convenient to 60 and 66

56

Old Tascosa Room, Herring Hotel

AMARILLO, TEXAS

1944

The Old Tascosa Room was a dine-and-dance nightclub in the Herring Hotel, which had been built in 1926 and was the largest and finest in downtown Amarillo. The club, which opened on September 19, 1942, offered meals, drinks, and dancing until 1967; after that it was converted to a bar until the building ceased operating as a hotel a few years later. The name for the nightspot came from the ghost town of Tascosa, the first substantial community in the Texas ranch country west of what later became Amarillo.

The fourteen-story Herring Hotel offered six hundred rooms, all with baths, at 319 Southeast Third Avenue, just half a block off U.S. Highway 66 along Fillmore Street. After surviving the hard times of the Great Depression, it experienced several years of full occupancy and good profits during World War II. Desiring to invest some of these earnings, owner Ernest O. Thompson hired Amarillo architect Guy A. Carlander to design the Old Tascosa supper club, which he placed in the basement level. About the same time Thompson commissioned nationally known cowboy artist Harold D. Bugbee to paint a series of murals in the room depicting scenes of ranch life; the fixtures and other décor chosen for the room, too, were reminiscent of the Old West.

Accordionist June Partell and fiddler Tommy Decker, who performed on national hotel and nightclub circuits, helped open the Old Tascosa Room in 1942. After the war, local trumpet player William "Schnozz" Dunn and his combo were regulars at the dinner club. A World War II–era menu gives some idea of the meals served at Old Tascosa: sandwiches made from roast beef, ham, or cheese at 35¢ apiece, pork chops with trimmings for $1.25, and "one and one-half inch thick" sirloin steaks for $2.00. Domestic beers sold for 13¢ to 18¢ a bottle, while dinner wine could be purchased for 45¢ a glass. The cover charge was a dollar.

The McCormick advertising agency in Amarillo ordered twenty-five thousand color postcards of the Old Tascosa Room in the Herring Hotel based on this photograph and others plus a drawing of a cowboy with a lasso prepared by artist Harold D. Bugbee. The printing job was assigned Curt Teich and Company stock number 4B-H1239 on November 1, 1944.

57

The Aristocrat Restaurant

AMARILLO, TEXAS

1946

The Aristocrat was a downtown eatery in Amarillo, Texas, directly fronting on the south side of U.S. Highway 66 at 119 West Sixth Street. Its location just around a corner from Polk Street, the main commercial thoroughfare in the city, gave it a reliable customer base of businesspeople and shoppers in addition to motorists on the cross-country highway.

Mickey Wood established the Aristocrat during the late summer of 1945, opening its doors on September 1. Her eating place offered diners the choice of table or counter service and provided air-conditioning, which was considered particularly modern at the time. Wood served breakfast, lunch, and dinner and was reported to go out of her way to prepare fresh vegetables, rolls, and muffins to accompany main dishes. A year after the restaurant opened, the local press observed that it attracted out-of-town customers, many of whom "make it a point to reach the Aristocrat for their luncheon or dinners."

Not long after opening her downtown café, Mickey Wood married Tillman H. McCafferty, and the couple ran the business together until the early 1950s, when the city directory showed that Mickey assumed the full managerial duties. The businesswoman had greater ambitions, however, and in 1952 opened a short-lived Mickey's Club, a tavern on Route 66 at 4936 Northeast Eighth Avenue (later Amarillo Boulevard East). She closed the Aristocrat Restaurant about 1956, but is known later to have operated two other eating places under the name of Mickey's Café adjacent to the Amarillo Truck Stop on the south side of Amarillo and at 2103 West Seventh Street, a block off U.S. Highway 66.

The McCormick Advertising Company in Amarillo ordered 12,500 color postcards showing the interior of the Aristocrat based on this photograph. In Chicago Curt Teich and Company gave the order stock number 6B-H264 on March 1, 1946, and its employees produced the cards.

5⅛   9⁵⁄₁₆

THE ARISTOCRAT — PHONE 23111 — 119 W. SIXTH AVE.

ON U. S. HIGHWAY 66 — AMARILLO, TEXAS

135

58

Cunningham Floral Company

AMARILLO, TEXAS

1937

With a glass-roofed display room built on to its front, Cunningham Floral Company at 2511 West Sixth Street was for years the preeminent greenhouse, nursery, and cut flower source in Amarillo, Texas. It fronted directly on the south side of the Sixth Street alignment of U.S. Highway 66 in the edge of the once fashionable San Jacinto Heights section of the city.

Charles Crews Cunningham and his wife, Carrie, came to Amarillo from Comanche, Texas, in 1902. After doing other work for a while, Charles began a plant nursery at 111 East Fourth. He and Carrie expanded it into a cut flower shop that initially operated out of their home. The retail outlet then moved downtown to 716 Polk Street, and the couple erected larger greenhouses at 2407 West Sixth. When these proved inadequate, they erected even larger glass houses a block away at 2511 West Sixth. The retail flower shop in 1926 shifted from downtown to a location adjacent to the new hothouses.

The floral company raised most of its own flowers and potted plants, but it shipped in some that were less expensive to purchase than to grow. The most popular year-round flowers were roses. "Although there are lots of varieties and colors," Carrie Cunningham stated in 1941, "nearly everybody asks for red ones." She noted that the shop received more orders in general for sick-room bouquets than any other cut flowers.

William J. Beechler, a Milwaukee florist, joined the Amarillo business in 1922. Two years later Charles Cunningham died in his mid-forties, and his widow, Carrie, sold a share of the enterprise to Beechler and his wife, Jessie. The three partners operated Cunningham Floral for the next two dozen years, adding the attractive glassed-in showroom depicted in the photograph. In time Mrs. Cunningham and the Beechlers retired, selling the enterprise to others who operated it under the old name into the 1980s. At the time of writing, the building housed a tavern, its parking area occupying the site of the former greenhouses behind the store.

Cunningham Floral Company sent this photograph with an order for 12,500 color postcards to Curt Teich and Company. On its arrival in Chicago, the job was given stock number 7A-H549, and work began on February 12, 1937. The customer stated that the floral display in the black-and-white photo consisted mainly of chrysanthemums but asked the artists in Chicago to "fill up blank spaces with additional ferns, palms or suggestions of other types of flowers."

LARGEST AND MOST MODERN FLORAL ESTABLISHMENT IN NORTHWEST TEXAS

2511 WEST SIXTH AVENUE ～ PHONE: 8259 ～ AMARILLO, TEXAS   7A-H549

Sunset Motel

AMARILLO, TEXAS

1951

The Sunset Motel came into existence because of the rerouting of U.S. Highway 66 away from the downtown business district of Amarillo. For decades the roadway entered the city from the east along Northeast Eighth Avenue and then dropped south via Fillmore Street through the main commercial district. Once there the road turned westward on West Sixth Street and proceeded out of the city toward New Mexico. This alignment brought all of the cross-country traffic of the main east–west highway right through the increasingly congested heart of the city.

After the close of World War II, officials of the Texas Highway Department consulted with leaders in Amarillo on how to resolve the traffic problems. Together they came up with a plan to divert the highway completely around the central business district by extending Eighth Street westward in four lanes all the way to a traffic circle near the 1940 Veterans Hospital and thence along the established route out of the city. No sooner were the plans made than entrepreneurs began erecting new motels and eating places along the projected new alignment, the name of which later changed to Amarillo Boulevard. This construction included the Sunset Motel.

Even before pavement was laid in front of the site, Joe K. and Eula Williams in 1950 erected the Sunset Motel at 5703 West U.S. 66. It had a two-story office with a manager's apartment upstairs, and twenty motel units laid

out in a U shape with a landscaped courtyard and children's playground in the center. Guests enjoyed the comfort of air-conditioning during the summer and individual furnaces for wintertime heating. A customer in 1959 wrote home on a motel postcard, "This really is a nice place but picture is terrible. Nice steak house next door." Business at the Sunset Motel remained strong until cross-country traffic shifted to Interstate 40 in 1968. Even before that occurred, a changing series of owners led to inconsistent management. The name switched from Sunset Motel to Medical Manor Motel to Budget Motel and finally to Astro Motel, under which name it occasionally housed guests at the time of writing.

The McCormick advertising firm in Amarillo ordered 12,500 color postcards based on these photographs for Mr. and Mrs. Joe K. Williams at the Sunset Motel. Curt Teich and Company on January 12, 1951, assigned the job stock number 1C-H39, and when creating the card its artists added a decorative sunburst in the upper left corner.

LA BAJADA HILL, BETWEEN SANTA FE AND ALBUQUERQUE, NEW MEXICO   121023

CHAPTER SIX

NEW MEXICO

FOR A SHORT DISTANCE INTO NEW MEXICO, motorists drove atop the flat plains, but quickly the road dropped off down an escarpment leading toward the Pecos River. The two-lane U.S. 66 took them toward Tucumcari and then to Santa Rosa, where they crossed the river.

From just west of Santa Rosa, the highway initially headed north and then west to Santa Fe, the state capital, founded in about 1608. This route took them over the Glorieta Pass, scene of an 1862 battle between Confederate Texans and Union Coloradoans and New Mexicans. In that immediate area Thomas L. Greer purchased an adobe ranch house in the 1920s and created a roadside attraction: together with a menagerie and Civil War relics, he featured a hand-dug well he advertised (erroneously) as the oldest in America. Once in Santa Fe, motorists who could afford the luxury stayed at La Fonda Hotel, operated by the Fred Harvey Company, and toured the Pueblo Indian villages and ruins in the area. The old 66 roadway then turned south to Albuquerque by way of La Bajada Hill, a five-hundred-foot drop with twenty-six tight switchbacks down into the valley of the Rio Grande and thence downstream to Albuquerque.

In 1937 a new road was constructed westward from Santa Rosa along a more direct route to Albuquerque, cutting off Santa Fe and thereby shortening the distance from Chicago to Los Angeles by seventy-five miles. It took travelers down the Tijeras Canyon and directly into Albuquerque, the largest city in New Mexico. There they found perhaps even more American Indians than they had seen in Oklahoma. At Maisel's Indian Trading Post, fronting on U.S. 66 along Central Avenue, they could watch Indian silversmiths crafting distinctive southwestern jewelry. Many eating places offered New Mexican–style foods, but those who wanted simpler fare often went to Katson's Drive-In for hamburgers and fries.

Westward from Albuquerque drivers passed through more Pueblo Indian country before entering the lands of the Navajos around Gallup and Grants. Huge red rocks emerged from the ground, creating exotic landscapes unlike anything many travelers had seen except in cowboy movies. In this bizarre, arid land they found scattered trading posts where Native people bartered weavings, pottery, and jewelry for groceries, clothing, and fuel. Often these stores were the only stops motorists could find. Except where the road took drivers up to areas with enough elevation to trap the scarce precipitation, the landscape was barren and dry. Through such country just beyond Gallup, the 66 Highway took travelers across the border into Arizona.

60

Aerial View of Tucumcari

NEW MEXICO

1940

An aerial photograph provided this image of Tucumcari that J. R. Willis of Albuquerque sent to Curt Teich and Company when he ordered 12,500 postcards in the summer of 1940. Dominating the view was Tucumcari Mountain, the flat-topped mesa that greeted U.S. Highway 66 travelers before they could glimpse the town near its base. This erosional remnant gave the community its name, which is believed to come from a Comanche word meaning "to lie in wait for someone or something to approach."

After the impressive Tucumcari Mountain, the next most visible feature of Tucumcari from the air was its railway line, seen in the foreground of the picture. It was this railroad that breathed life into the town, which began in 1902 as a railway construction camp on a Rock Island Railroad line that connected Liberal, Kansas, with Santa Rosa, New Mexico. There it met lines from El Paso and California. Known initially as Six Shooter Siding from the violence in the construction camp, the town named itself Tucumcari, after the mountain, about 1902 and grew into a respectable city. The Rock Island Railroad constructed a new depot for Tucumcari in 1926, and that building, easily seen beside the tracks in the photograph, at the time of writing was being renovated to serve as a new Tucumcari Rail Museum.

Local automobile drivers in the 1910s tended to go from one side of Tucumcari to the other by using an already established route along unpaved Gaynell Avenue through a residential district. This way they avoided delays occasioned by passing through the downtown district next to the railroad tracks. Gaynell Avenue (later Tucumcari Boulevard) in 1926 was designated as the alignment for U.S. Highway 66 across the town. The thoroughfare courses east and west about eight blocks south of the railway depot.

Curt Teich and Company received this photograph with a request for 12,500 color postcards on June 5, 1940, from distributor J. R. Willis in Albuquerque, New Mexico. The printer gave it stock number 0B-H1181.

61

U.S. Highway 66 through Tucumcari

NEW MEXICO

1952

The alignment that U.S. Highway 66 took east–west across Tucumcari, New Mexico, was along Gaynell Avenue (later Tucumcari Boulevard), at first a predominantly residential district. As the number of motorists increased over the years and the lots fronting on the roadway became increasingly valuable as commercial property, businesses serving travelers gradually pushed out most of the homeowners. By the time this photograph was made in the early 1950s, efforts had been made to improve U.S. 66 on both sides of Tucumcari as well as through the town. The two-lane avenue was widened to four lanes, with a raised concrete median down the center.

Even though Tucumcari had its own basic economy and identity, Route 66 motorists knew it from the Gaynell Avenue business strip as the "town two streets wide and five miles long." For out-of-town visitors, it seemed to offer nothing but gasoline stations, cafés, and tourist courts. Chamber of commerce billboards as far east as Texas and as far west as California advertised "Tucumcari Tonight" to promote the business activity along this ribbon of pavement, which in time competed with ranching and the railroad as major sources of income for the community.

The Southwest Post Card Company in Albuquerque sent this black-and-white photograph to Curt Teich and Company as the raw material for the production of a color postcard. The picture taken on the east side of town shows most clearly the 1000 block of Gaynell Avenue, as viewed looking west. At the left side of the image stands the Hayes Motor Company building at 1006 Gaynell, which at the time of writing survived as the Golden Dragon Restaurant. Beyond it on the left is Leland's Gulf service station at 925 Gaynell. In 1959 Leland's Gulf was remodeled and became the well-known Tee Pee Curios store, which had a concrete teepee fused onto its front.

On the right side of the street is a row of motels, including La Plaza Motel (part of which still stands in the Roadrunner Motel) as well as the Yucca Motel and the Rainbow's End Court, neither of which survives. Indistinguishable just beyond these motels on the right, near a five-pointed-star Texaco filling station sign, is the widely known Blue Swallow Court. Although Tucumcari today abounds with significant Route 66 enterprises from the 1960s to the 1970s, one can still find roadside culture from earlier days.

This photograph reached Curt Teich and Company in Chicago by June 11, 1952, when it received stock number 2C-H786 and production began.

62

Two Bridges on the Pecos

SANTA ROSA, NEW MEXICO

1939

Traveling west on U.S. Highway 66, motorists began their descent into the Pecos River Valley when they dropped off the table-top flat plains at a distinct escarpment just after crossing the Texas–New Mexico state line. It was a hundred miles farther on, at Santa Rosa, that both the highway and the Rock Island Railroad actually went over the Pecos, a usually muddy watercourse.

The bridges spanning the Pecos at Santa Rosa were both built about the turn of the twentieth century. The railroad bridge was part of a larger project to connect Kansas City by rail with El Paso. As a segment of this line, the Chicago, Rock Island and Pacific (CRI&P) Railroad in 1901–1902 built from Liberal, Kansas, southwestward across the Oklahoma and Texas Panhandles to Santa Rosa. There it connected with newly constructed tracks of the El Paso and Northeastern Railroad from Carrizozo, New Mexico, which already linked with El Paso. At Santa Rosa the CRI&P erected a steel bridge spanning the Pecos that included three 80-foot spans and two 35-foot spans supported on riveted steel towers with a pair of stone abutments. This is the first and larger of the two bridges seen in the photograph, and it remains at this site. Beneath its west (right) end, present-day Serrano Drive at the time of writing still carried local traffic on historic pavement from former U.S. Highway 66.

Downstream the county constructed a nine-panel camelback-style overhead truss bridge to carry wagons and early automobiles across the waters of the Pecos. In the 1930s, after the routing of U.S. Highway 66 through Santa Rosa, this structure was replaced by the stronger concrete and steel stringer bridge seen in the photograph. This bridge also appeared in a scene of the 1940 film *The Grapes of Wrath*, directed by John Ford. It survived until 1959, when the current wider concrete and steel highway bridge took its place.

Curt Teich and Company received an order from distributor J. R. Willis in Albuquerque, New Mexico, on July 27, 1939, for 12,500 color postcards based on this photograph, assigning it stock number 9A-H1264.

Oldest Well in U.S.A.

GLORIETA PASS, NEW MEXICO

1931

The designation of U.S. Highway 66 as a cross-country highway created economic opportunities for local residents along its route. One of them was Thomas L. Greer, who earlier had operated a "Cowboy Park" tourist attraction in Juarez, Mexico. The U.S. highway initially followed the much older Santa Fe Trail over the Glorieta Pass about twenty miles from Santa Fe, and Greer purchased a lot at the site where Alexander Pigeon had operated a trailside lodging, store, and ranch in the 1860s. Pigeon's headquarters had been the scene of fighting during the Battle of Glorieta Pass (March 26–28, 1862) between invading Texan Confederate troops and U.S. Army troops and Union volunteers from New Mexico and Colorado.

The earliest alignment of Highway 66 led it northward from Santa Rosa, New Mexico, over the Glorieta Pass into Santa Fe and then looped southward down to Albuquerque. It passed directly in front of Pigeon's old adobe ranch headquarters, where in the late 1920s Thomas Greer created his own tourist attraction. For twenty-five cents the entrepreneur gave visitors guided tours of the "old hospital" from the Civil War battle, "old walls," and his "old Spanish fort," all of which were actually remnants of Pigeon's Ranch. Greer also promoted a hand-dug water well on the opposite side of the road as "the oldest well in the United States," even though it was documented as existing no earlier than 1867.

Out of curiosity traveling journalists Ilya Ilf and Eugene Petrov visited Greer's Glorieta Pass site in 1936. Attracted by a sign reading, "Your grandfather drank water here on his way to California for gold," they found a man in a booth selling colored postcards illustrating the well. More interesting to the visitors were two bears "begging the travelers for gifts" that the businessman had chained to a post driven into the ground. Greer's tourist attraction suffered when the alignment of U.S. Highway 66 diverted away from Glorieta Pass in 1937 to a more direct east–west connection between Santa Rosa and Albuquerque. The roadside business finally closed permanently in the 1950s. In 1990 ownership of the property passed to the Pecos National Monument, and at the time of writing the old well remained in existence behind a two-foot stone retaining wall at the southwest side of New Mexico State Highway 50 near its intersection with Pigeon Ranch Road.

Early in 1931 Thomas L. Greer ordered 12,500 color postcards showing his "historic" well; he enclosed this photograph as the artwork. The mailing reached Chicago by January 7, 1931, when Curt Teich and Company employees assigned it stock number F14921 and began the printing process.

Color match

Oldest Well in U. S. A.   Most Historic and Wonderful Old Indian-Spanish Well

Under Management of Thos. L. Greer, Glorieta Pass, N. Mex.   114921-N

La Fonda Hotel

SANTA FE, NEW MEXICO

1933

Considered one of the truly unique hotels in the United States, La Fonda in Santa Fe opened in 1922 at 100 East San Francisco Street just off the central plaza where travelers had lodged at least since the days of the Santa Fe Trail in the early nineteenth century. Architect Isaac Rapp designed the building in 1919 in the Pueblo Spanish style that had developed in Santa Fe. The form incorporated traditional Indian and Spanish Colonial elements, including flat roofs; massive, round-cornered adobe-looking walls; timber beams supporting ceilings; and carved wooden corbels at the tops of timber posts.

La Fonda operated under local management until its purchase in 1925 by the Atchison, Topeka and Santa Fe Railway. The next year the railroad leased it to the Fred Harvey Company, which ran it for the next forty years. The latter firm since the 1870s had operated eating places and later hotels alongside the Santa Fe tracks. The Harvey Company in 1926 began a three-year expansion of La Fonda to accommodate more guests, adding about fifty-five rooms and a decorative fifth-floor bell tower. This construction gave the building the appearance seen in the photograph.

Many notable guests, including several U.S. presidents, have enjoyed the quiet pleasures of La Fonda. Aviator Charles A. Lindbergh overnighted there during a cross-country trip by air in 1927 following his first successful solo flight across the Atlantic. Author Willa Cather resided there while she worked on the manuscript for her novel *Death Comes for the Archbishop*, which was based on the life of Bishop Jean-Baptiste Lamy of Santa Fe. During the premiere of the 1940 film *Santa Fe Trail*, actors Errol Flynn and Olivia de Havilland stayed in the hotel. It remains a popular place to stay in Santa Fe for many travelers, including heritage tourists retracing the route of former U.S. Highway 66.

During the fall of 1933, distributor Southwest Arts & Crafts in Santa Fe placed an order for 12,500 color postcards based on this heavily retouched black-and-white photograph taken by T. H. Parkhurst. The order reached Curt Teich and Company by October 24, 1933, and went into production as stock number 3A-H1067.

5 9/16 square

PHOTO BY T. H. PARKHURST

H-4480   LA FONDA, THE INN AT THE END OF THE TRAIL, IN SANTA FE, NEW MEXICO

65

The Patio, La Fonda Hotel

SANTA FE, NEW MEXICO

1937

Architect Isaac Rapp designed La Fonda Hotel around an open courtyard, a feature of many of the upper-class Spanish Colonial homes in New Mexico. In these traditional residences many of the rooms opened onto a central patio area. At La Fonda the courtyard served as an extension of the bar so that guests could take their beverages outside during mild weather and sit either in the sunshine or beneath umbrellas at tables. A kitchen operated behind the doors at the right side, so guests also had the option of dining in the open air. It was not unusual for small combos of Hispanic musicians to perform in the patio, the strains of their tunes wafting upward to the open windows of guest rooms that overlooked the space.

The bar and eating places at La Fonda for decades were the most popular meeting places for the elites in Santa Fe. Journalist Ernie Pyle visited the city in the early 1930s and found that "life among the upper crust centered by daytime in the La Fonda Hotel." He added, "You could go there any time of day and see a few artists at the bar, or an Indian that some white woman loved, or a goateed nobleman from Austria, or a maharaja from India, or a New York broker, or an archaeologist, or some local light in overalls and cowboy boots. You never met anybody anywhere except at La Fonda."

In 1975 the operators of La Fonda Hotel placed a glass roof atop the patio area and turned it into La Plazuela Restaurant; they retained the tiers of artistically painted glass windows in the wooden doors and walls. At the same time the level of guest rooms that had overlooked the patio on the second floor was converted to a mezzanine. Later, in 2008, the operators reconstructed the circular fountain that earlier had graced the center of the former patio. At the time of writing, La Fonda Hotel staff were serving meals in La Plazuela at breakfast, lunch, and dinner, and it continued to attract a wide clientele of locals and out-of-town visitors.

In early 1937 distributor J. R. Willis in Albuquerque, New Mexico, placed an order for 12,500 color postcards based on this black-and-white photograph of the interior courtyard at La Fonda Hotel. Willis noted that he had received the photograph from the Fred Harvey Company and requested that the card be identified with Harvey number H-4220. Curt Teich and Company personnel in Chicago received the order by January 27, 1937, when they assigned the job stock number 7A-H307 and began production.

H-4220   THE PATIO, LA FONDA HOTEL, SANTA FE, NEW MEXICO

66

The Indian Room, La Fonda Hotel

SANTA FE, NEW MEXICO

1937

The Fred Harvey Company had a symbiotic relationship with the Atchison, Topeka and Santa Fe Railway. Harvey operated eating places and later hotels along tracks of the Santa Fe, which stopped its trains for passengers' rest stops. This meant that the railroad for decades saved money by not having to own and run so many expensive dining cars on its trains.

By the turn of the twentieth century, Fred Harvey conceived the idea of marketing the Desert Southwest as an exotic destination for tourists, who at the time still traveled predominantly by train. Promoting the culture of indigenous American Indians formed a major part of this corporate strategy. The Harvey firm established its "Indian Department" in 1901 as a means of retailing the arts and crafts of Native Americans. The next year the company opened an Indian Building adjacent to its downtown railway station and hotel complex in Albuquerque, and in 1905 it created the Hopi House commercial outlet at the Grand Canyon. More such merchandising was to follow.

No sooner did the company lease La Fonda from the Santa Fe Railway in 1926 than it opened an Indian Room in the hotel. There one could purchase indigenous arts and crafts: handwoven rugs, silver jewelry, beadwork, pottery, baskets, and more. As the Harvey Company expanded its operations to additional hotels in New Mexico and Arizona, each new enterprise incorporated retail areas devoted to Native arts. Although the Fred Harvey Company had long ceased to manage La Fonda Hotel, at the time of writing Indian arts and crafts remained a significant part of the retail trade in the historic inn.

In January 1937 postcard distributor J. R. Willis in Albuquerque, New Mexico, ordered 12,500 color postcards showing the Indian Room at La Fonda Hotel in Santa Fe; he enclosed this photograph. Curt Teich and Company employees in Chicago assigned the printing job stock number 7A-H306 on January 27, 1937.

Guest Room, La Fonda Hotel

SANTA FE, NEW MEXICO

1937

Almost as soon as it purchased La Fonda Hotel in 1925 and leased it to the Fred Harvey Company the next year, the Santa Fe Railway Company began expanding the facility to house more guests. This construction was part of an overall collaborative strategy of the two firms to create hotels that could serve as hubs for tourists visiting scenic and cultural attractions by way of motor coaches known as "Harveycars." They marketed the bus excursions from the hotels as Indian Detours.

From Harvey hotels in Santa Fe and Albuquerque, sightseers rode open-window coaches to the Pueblo Indian villages conveniently located in the Rio Grande Valley. From Gallup, New Mexico, they visited Canyon de Chelly, Zuni Pueblo, the Inscription Rock, and Mesa Verde. Farther to the west, from Winslow, Arizona, the tourists went by "Harveycars" to view the Painted Desert, the Petrified Forest, and the Meteor Crater. The Grand Canyon, with its own Harvey hotels and on a branch line of the Santa Fe Railway, was an attraction in itself. The opening of U.S. Highway 66 brought even more potential customers.

The photograph shows one of the guest rooms constructed at La Fonda in Santa Fe during a 1926–27 expansion. The interiors were all designed by architect Mary Jane Colter, whom Fred Harvey first employed in 1901. All the furnishings for La Fonda guest rooms were custom-made according to Colter's specifications and were hand-painted in Santa Fe. An Associated Press account in 1929 detailed, "In one room the design embodying a bull fight, which is found hand-painted on the front of the dresser, is repeated in the rug in front of the dresser. Again the design on a rug which lies between twin beds is the same as the design on the bed heads." Even the blanket boxes and the shades on the bedside lamps were individually painted; each room had its own thematic unity. At the time of writing, many of these furnishings remained in service at La Fonda, and some of the small historic headboards were exhibited along corridors as works of art.

Albuquerque postcard distributor J. R. Willis placed an order for 12,500 color postcards based on this retouched black-and-white photograph showing a La Fonda Hotel guest room. His order and photograph reached Chicago by January 27, 1937, the day that Curt Teich and Company employees gave it stock number 7A-H309 and initiated production.

F. W. Woolworth Company Building

SANTA FE, NEW MEXICO

1939

Ever since Santa Fe was founded about 1608, the rectangular plaza at its center has been the heart of the community. The city grew around this space: it was not only where the elites erected their homes, but also served as the central marketplace for food, livestock, and forage. When Mexico won its independence from Spain in 1821, the square was renamed the Plaza de la Constitucion, and it became the destination for American traders coming in freight wagons down the Santa Fe Trail. It was here that General Stephen W. Kearney declared the annexation of New Mexico to the United States in 1846. Merchants replaced most of the old residences with commercial buildings in the 1880s. It is still a place for buying and selling.

Starting in 1935 and for decades, the F. W. Woolworth's Company operated a variety store inside two and later three of the storefronts on San Francisco Street at the south side of the plaza in Santa Fe. It became a beloved local institution. Here customers could buy suntan lotion, T-shirts, balloons, chewing gum, and many other inexpensive items in one of the largest-grossing Woolworth's stores in the entire nation. In 1997, after years of losses in other locations due to competition, Woolworth Corporation announced it would close all of its remaining stores, including the one on the Santa Fe Plaza.

Local entrepreneurs Earl Potter and Mike Collins saw opportunity in the closing of the store. They developed a plan to market the former store's best-selling merchandise in a third of the space formerly occupied by larger Woolworth's, calling the new enterprise the Five & Dime General Store. There they sold such everyday items as sunglasses, postcards, hats, toothbrushes, and cosmetics, and their business plan succeeded even better than they had expected. At the time of writing, the Five & Dime General Store concept had expanded into eight different cities around the country.

On December 8, 1939, Curt Teich and Company received an order from distributor J. R. Willis in Albuquerque, New Mexico, for sixty-five hundred color postcards of the F. W. Woolworth Company store in Santa Fe. The order included this slightly retouched black-and-white photograph of the store as it appeared at the end of the Great Depression. Teich employees began production and assigned the job stock number 9A-H2390.

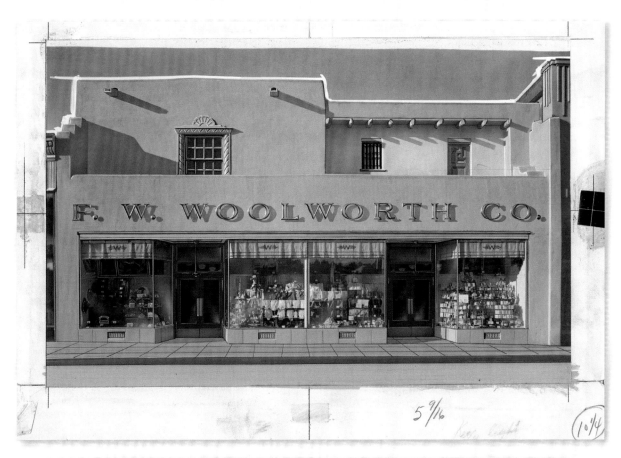

La Bajada Hill

BETWEEN SANTA FE

AND

ALBUQUERQUE, NEW MEXICO

1928

Motorists driving the original route of U.S. Highway 66 between Santa Fe and Albuquerque found themselves traversing a substantial natural barrier. About fifteen miles southwest of Santa Fe the gravel highway came to the edge of a high volcanic escarpment known as La Bajada, "The Descent." There an east–west basalt cliff dropped off about five hundred feet into the valley of the Rio Grande.

The gravel roadway up and down the steep slope was cut in 1922 by Indian workers hired from Cochiti Pueblo along with prisoners from the state penitentiary. Motorists faced twenty-six switchbacks at an 8 percent grade. When they approached the drop-off at the top of the hill, drivers read a signpost ominously alerting them, "This road is not fool proof, but safe for a sane driver." Travel writer Vernon McGill in 1922 described the switch-backs as looking "like a snake in motion." Travelers continued this route up and down La Bajada Hill until 1932, when U.S. 66 shifted three miles to the east, to a gentler but still steep slope.

In the winter of 1926–27, nature writer Dallas Lore Sharp passed over La Bajada Hill on an overland trip from Boston to California. At its crest he found a car full of people that had not made even the first switchback. "The driver . . . had cut too slow, and stood, with cramped wheels and locked brakes, on the brink of a terrifying wall," he wrote. Sharp jumped out to assist the terrified driver. "Only . . . quick, cool, coördinate action between release brakes and reverse gears could clutch the narrow leavings of that . . . ledge and back safely off the precipice." The day was saved, and both cars before long made their way down the multiple hairpin turns.

On June 4, 1928, an order from the Southwest Arts & Crafts store in Santa Fe for twelve thousand color postcards based on this photograph reached Curt Teich and Company. Employees there assigned the job stock number 121023 and began production.

LA BAJADA HILL, BETWEEN SANTA FE AND ALBUQUERQUE, NEW MEXICO   121023

U.S. 66 Four-Lane Highway through Tijeras Canyon

EAST OF ALBUQUERQUE,

NEW MEXICO

1952

The initial alignment of U.S. Highway 66 between Santa Rosa and Albuquerque took a big loop northward and then westward to Santa Fe via Glorieta Pass and then southward down the Rio Grande Valley to Albuquerque. Then in 1937 the state with federal assistance constructed a more direct east–west connection between Santa Rosa and Albuquerque. This new road carried traffic west through Moriarty and then down through a natural pass called Tijeras Canyon into the Rio Grande Valley at Albuquerque. The new route shortened the distance between Chicago and Los Angeles by about seventy-five miles.

The 1937 realignment of Highway 66 took it as a roadway through the Tijeras Canyon. This gap constituted one of the few natural east–west passes through the generally north–south Sandia and Manzano Mountains, which lie directly east of Albuquerque. The highway paralleled a preexisting wagon road and a 1920s gravel "tourist road" through the pass. The steep-walled valley had been home to prehistoric Puebloan Indians and later to historic tribes and Spanish colonial settlers, but by the 1930s a series of villages lay in its bottom and along its sides. As soon as cross-country motorists began coursing through the area, a number of filling stations, roadside camps, and bars sprang up, and in time the area filled with urban sprawl and the 1950s concrete plant that now visually dominates part of the area.

The old two-lane 1937 alignment of Route 66 through Tijeras Canyon was widened in 1951, and that four-lane thoroughfare is depicted on the photograph. The roadway continued to serve U.S. Highway 66 traffic until it was bypassed by construction of Interstate 40 on a significantly built-up roadbed that carries the majority of motorists through the canyon today. Much of the old 66 pavement survives through the canyon and can be driven by those who seek it out.

In early winter of 1952, just after Highway 66 had been widened through Tijeras Canyon, the Southwest Post Card Company in Albuquerque sent this photograph of the improved highway to Curt Teich and Company as the basis for an order of twenty-five thousand color postcards. On February 7, 1952, the Chicago publisher's employees initiated production, assigning the card stock number 2C-H208.

Alvarado Hotel

ALBUQUERQUE, NEW MEXICO

1939

The Alvarado was the first truly luxurious hotel in Albuquerque. It also was the first large hotel constructed by the Santa Fe Railway for the Fred Harvey Company after the two firms began promoting cultural tourism in the American Southwest. Erected in 1901–1902, the hotel adjoined the Santa Fe depot in the heart of downtown on First Street at Central Avenue, which later became U.S. Highway 66 through the city.

The Santa Fe Railway and its food-vending partner, the Fred Harvey Company, gambled that they both would profit if they could attract tourists to the Desert Southwest as an exotic destination. Together they promoted the scenic beauties of areas where the Santa Fe tracks passed, like the Grand Canyon and the Petrified Forest, and constructed facilities to serve travelers who visited them. Soon after erecting the Alvarado Hotel in Albuquerque, for example, the railway began construction of El Tovar Hotel on the south rim of the Grand Canyon. The railroad delivered customers, and the Fred Harvey Company cared for them once they arrived.

The Fred Harvey Company operated its first retail outlet for southwestern Indian arts and crafts next door to the Alvarado Hotel. In addition to eating meals in the hotel, during rest stops in Albuquerque train passengers could step inside the trackside Indian Building to watch native people weaving rugs, crafting silver jewelry, and making baskets, with plenty of examples available for sale. By the mid-1920s the Alvarado became one of several hubs for the Indian Detour trips by motor coach. With personable young women as guides, these excursions took tourists to visit Pueblo villages in the Rio Grande Valley, where they could interact with American Indians in home settings.

The Alvarado Hotel stood until 1970, when the Santa Fe Railway Company demolished the complex. The site remained vacant for years, but in the 2000s it became the location for the present-day Alvarado Transportation Center, which serves rail and bus traffic in downtown Albuquerque.

The Fred Harvey Company in Chicago, Illinois, ordered six thousand color postcards of the Alvarado Hotel just after the start of the new year in 1939. The order was received by Curt Teich and Company on January 11, 1939. There the job received stock number 9A-H61 and Fred Harvey Company number H-4476, after which it went into production.

5⅛

⑨

H-4476—CENTRAL PATIO, THE FRED HARVEY-ALVARADO HOTEL, ALBUQUERQUE, NEW MEXICO

KiMo Theater

A new entertainment medium, the motion picture, swept across the United States during the first quarter of the twentieth century. In 1900 there was not a single building devoted exclusively to commercial screening of motion pictures in America, but by the mid-1920s there were thousands of them. Some of these facilities were truly movie palaces, and the KiMo was one of these remarkable public spaces.

In 1925 local Italian American entrepreneur Oreste Bachechi conceived the idea for constructing a large, luxurious downtown movie house in Albuquerque. He already operated other theaters in the city and knew the business, but realized he needed help to create the auditorium he envisioned. Bachechi hired architect Carl Boller, whose New York City firm specialized in theaters, to design a movie house that would combine Pueblo Spanish Revival designs with the Art Deco ornamentation that was highly fashionable at the time. The resulting combined Pueblo Deco building was a magnificent success, melding the stepped-back massing, rounded corners, and adobe color of traditional southwestern architecture with angular, geometric elements popularized by the Arts Décoratifs movement.

Located at the busy northeast corner of Fifth Street with Central Avenue, the thoroughfare that in 1937 became Route 66 east–west through Albuquerque, the KiMo Theater opened to the public on September 19, 1927. Pablo Abeita, the American Indian governor of Isleta Pueblo, suggested its name from the Tewa word meaning "mountain lion," liberally translated as "king of its kind." The theater screened first-run motion pictures from the 1920s into the 1960s, when it closed during a general decline of downtown Albuquerque. In 1977 the citizens of Albuquerque approved the sale of bonds to purchase the movie palace, and in stages funded its restoration over the next quarter century. In 2011 a later-added but long-lost neon sign was reconstructed for its front. At the time of writing, the KiMo continued to operate as an active center for the performing arts.

About three months before the formal dedication of the KiMo, the Smith-Brooks Press of Denver, Colorado, which distributed postcards, sent this photograph with an order for twelve thousand color postcards showing the theater as originally built. Curt Teich and Company employees in Chicago started the printing process on July 22, 1927, and assigned the job stock number 115666.

KIMO, AMERICA'S FOREMOST INDIAN THEATRE, ALBUQUERQUE, NEW MEXICO   A-3

SEE OTHER SIDE

73

Indian Silversmiths from Maisel's Indian Trading Post

ALBUQUERQUE, NEW MEXICO

1938

Maurice M. Maisel was among the first individuals in the southwestern Indian arts and crafts trade to realize the potential for employing Native artisans to produce custom silver, stone, and shell jewelry as a means of supplying both retail and wholesale markets. Most traders in these materials at the time purchased their stock from individual craftsmen who brought in completed pieces of jewelry and then bargained over the prices. It was an innovation for a trader to hire craftspeople to make up pieces of jewelry in a workshop according to the employer's specifications.

Maisel entered the Indian arts trade in 1923 in Albuquerque and had ample opportunity to observe the growing role of U.S. Highway 66 in bringing increasing numbers of potential customers. Consequently in 1939 he erected a major retail outlet directly on the Mother Road at 510 Central Avenue Southwest in downtown Albuquerque. The store occupied a prime location diagonally across from the big KiMo motion picture theater and only four blocks from the Alvarado Hotel.

Maisel hired architect John Gaw Meem to draw up plans, then erected a retail space in a popular blend of Pueblo Spanish Revival architecture with trendy Art Deco that came to be known as Pueblo Deco style. Above its plate-glass show windows he placed a mural of southwestern Indians in ceremonial attire. Locally prominent artist Olive Rush designed the work, but Maisel hired young American Indian artists to paint the figures. This made his store the only Pueblo Deco building in Albuquerque that used actual paintings by Navajo and Pueblo artists. Inside the store customers could look down a staircase to more Indian artisans at work in the basement workshop producing jewelry for sale upstairs.

The downtown trading post closed after Maurice Maisel's death in 1968, but in the 1980s his grandson, Skip, reopened the store. At the time of writing, it was operating in the same location under the name Skip Maisel's Indian Jewelry and Crafts.

In autumn 1938 Maisel's Indian Trading Post in Albuquerque requested 12,500 color postcards showing almost three dozen of its Indian silversmiths dressed in stylized Native attire. The order reached Curt Teich and Company in Chicago by November 14, 1938, when it received stock number 8A-H2857 and work began on the printing job.

MAISEL'S INDIAN TRADING POST — ALBUQUERQUE, NEW MEXICO

SOME OF OUR INDIAN SILVERSMITHS ARE SHOWN HERE IN CEREMONIAL COSTUME

Katson's Drive-In

74

ALBUQUERQUE, NEW MEXICO

1941

One way the automobile changed the American dining experience was the proliferation of drive-in eating places, enterprises at which customers typically arrived in motor vehicles and were greeted by nattily uniformed employees, usually young people, who took orders for foods and beverages. Once these "carhops" delivered the order to the kitchen, other employees cooked and/or assembled quickly prepared foods and beverages, and the young couriers delivered them to the customers at their cars. There payment was made and employees might receive money tips for their services. Many of these restaurants also made available some inside dining as well.

From the Atlantic to the Pacific these drive-in eating places proliferated during the 1920s, and their numbers grew even more quickly in the 1930s and 1940s. Virtually every town of any size had at least one drive-in, and larger communities had lots of them.

Robert Virgil Katson operated the popular downtown Albuquerque Court Café and the Hickory Restaurant, but neither of them offered convenient parking or curb service. He realized that money could be made by having foods prepared quickly and delivered to cars by pretty girls. So on May 18, 1940, he opened Katson's Drive-In at 2425 West Central Avenue, fronting directly onto U.S. Highway 66 in the "motel district" west of downtown. "Albuquerque needs a modern drive-in food emporium to meet the streamlined service that other large cities are opening," read a newspaper advertisement the day the eatery opened. It added, "You may dine inside at a table or booth, lunch at the fountain or on the patio, or have your order delivered to your car." As good as the idea was, Katson's Drive-In did not last very long. Rationing of foods and supplies during World War II made it difficult for Robert Katson to secure everything he needed to run the eatery. As early as 1947 the former restaurateur had left food service and entered the jewelry business.

After it had been open for business about a year and a half, Katson's Drive-In placed an order for twenty-five thousand color postcards showing the restaurant at sunset. The mailing, which included this photograph, arrived at Curt Teich and Company by January 10, 1941, and on that date it went into production, receiving stock number 0B-H2633.

KATSON'S DRIVE-IN   ALBUQUERQUE, N. M.

75

Fourth of July Parade

GRANTS, NEW MEXICO

1936

As travelers coursed westward on U.S. Highway 66, Grants was one of the last sizable towns through which they passed in New Mexico on their way toward the Arizona state line. The community came into existence during construction of the Atlantic & Pacific Railroad (later Santa Fe Railway) in the 1880s. As the temporary end of the steel rails, for a while it became a shipping point of supplies for construction camps operated by three brothers named Grant, giving the place the name Grant's Camp.

Unlike some Route 66 communities, Grants seems to have thrived through changing times. By the early twentieth century it became a prosperous agricultural center, raising carrots and livestock that the railroad shipped to markets. Then in 1950 a Navajo Indian rancher discovered what later was recognized as one of the largest uranium deposits in the world. For the next thirty years the town boomed as the home base for mining companies and their employees. Uranium production wound down during the early 1980s, but Grants remained busy, in part due to Route 66 heritage tourists and boaters and fishermen attracted by area reservoirs.

Since 1927 Grants has hosted an annual Independence Day amateur rodeo that draws contestants from around the American Southwest. Usually a three-day event that ends on the Fourth of July, it has featured a downtown parade since its beginning. The arena moved south of Grants when its earlier location in town became the site for a new high school.

For decades the 1920s Yucca Hotel served as the social center for Grants residents, as well as providing lodging for visitors arriving by train or automobile. Its affable manager, Greek American George Ade, also operated a motion picture theater, and many people viewed him as the town's unofficial "mayor." The 1940 American Automobile Association *Western Tour Book* noted that the hotel had fifty rooms, thirty-five of which had their own private baths, with double rooms from $1.75 to $2.50 a night. A local resident remembered that the Yucca typically housed travelers, railroad workers, loggers, and buyers of cattle, sheep, and produce during the carrot-harvesting season. The building in the 1100 block of West Santa Fe Avenue (Route 66) also housed such enterprises as a bar, restaurant, and jewelry store, and also served as a bus station. The facility survived into the 1960s, when it was torn down to make way for a western-wear store.

On December 16, 1936, Curt Teich and Company received an order from distributor J. R. Willis in Albuquerque for 12,500 color postcards showing mounted horsemen riding past the Yucca Hotel in the Fourth of July rodeo parade in Grants. Teich employees assigned the job stock number 6A-H2778 and began converting the black-and-white photograph, which they retouched, into a printed color postcard.

El Navajo Hotel

GALLUP, NEW MEXICO

1937

From 1902 to 1948, American architect Mary Jane Colter designed many of the hotels, eating places, and other tourist facilities built by the Santa Fe Railway and then leased to the Fred Harvey Company to operate. One of the most significant structures she designed was the El Navajo hotel and restaurant complex erected in 1923 adjacent to a preexisting depot at Gallup, New Mexico. Historians recognize this innovative structure as the most important early building designed in the Pueblo Deco style.

During the early twentieth century an architectural school emerged in Santa Fe, New Mexico, that revived elements of the Pueblo Indian and Spanish Colonial building styles. It emphasized rounded corners, stepped-back massing of walls, and the brown adobe color. Then in the 1920s artists and designers began to be influenced by the Art Deco style originating in Europe, known for its use of geometric shapes like zigzags, trapezoids, and circles. The two forms came together in the work of Mary Jane Colter and others in the Southwest in what came to be known as Pueblo Deco. The KiMo Theater in Albuquerque was a slightly later example of this same fusion of styles.

One important role the El Navajo Hotel played for the Fred Harvey Company was as a hub for its Indian Detour sightseeing tours. Starting in 1926, passengers detrained at Gallup to visit such attractions as Canyon de Chelly, Mesa Verde, Zuni Pueblo, the Inscription Rock, and the Navajo Country. Special motor coaches called "Harveycars" and large automobiles including Cadillacs, Packards, and Franklins transported them from their lodgings at El Navajo to see the places of interest; commentaries were given by personable young women tour guides.

Even though rail travel declined after World War II, El Navajo continued to serve the public until 1957, when it closed. That same year the hotel and restaurant portions of the large building complex were razed in part to make way for widening of U.S. Highway 66, which passed directly by the facility. After this demolition only the two buildings at the extreme left end of the photograph were standing. They survive today as the Gallup Cultural Center and a reduced-size station serving travelers on Amtrak passenger trains.

The Fred Harvey Company in Kansas City, Missouri, ordered six thousand color postcards of El Navajo in 1937. The packet of materials including this photograph arrived at Curt Teich and Company by February 22, 1937, when it was given stock number 7A-H646 and Fred Harvey Company number H-1892. Artists in Chicago heavily retouched the black-and-white photograph, which itself reproduced a painting by Fred Geary, as part of their work to create the color postcard.

Trimm exactly

5 · 3/16

H-1892   EL NAVAJO, FRED HARVEY HOTEL, GALLUP, NEW MEXICO (AFTER PAINTING BY FRED GEARY)

The Lobby, El Navajo Hotel

GALLUP, NEW MEXICO

1938

When people in the 1920s first entered the lobby of El Navajo Hotel in Gallup either from trains on one side or from Route 66 on the other, they saw an interior unlike any they had ever viewed before. The dazzling super-modern Art Deco interior unexpectedly combined with some of the finest traditional American Indian arts and crafts in the country. This was just the effect that architect Mary Jane Colter envisioned when she designed the building complex in 1916, even though its construction had to wait until after World War I in 1923.

El Navajo was the first public space in America where leaders of the Navajo Nation agreed to permit the display of images drawn from their ceremonial sand paintings. Navajo people believe that the *yei* spirits portrayed in these sand paintings actively mediate between people on the surface of the earth and the Great Spirit. This exhibition of sacred figures was such a major event for the Navajo people that three of their oldest medicine men performed a special blessing ritual for the facility when the hotel opened. Mary Jane Colter enhanced the effect of the sand-painting representations through the use of special lighting, tile floors, leather-upholstered furnishings, and American Indian arts, including Navajo rugs and Pueblo pottery.

When Englishman Mark Pepys visited El Navajo in the fall of 1935, he was less impressed by its décor than by the egalitarian atmosphere he encountered in its coffee shop. According to the visitor, Gallup "boasted a most excellent Fred Harvey house . . . [with] a menu of amazing variety." He went on to report, "Everyone sat along a huge counter: workmen, clerks, a cultured half-breed and tourists like ourselves. I like this. Had the governor of the State walked in, or the president of the whole country, I felt that both would have received the same service and no one would have looked more than twice at them." Pepys, who held a noble title as the Sixth Earl of Cottenham, could hardly believe the social equality he found among the diners that chance had thrown together in the hotel located between the Santa Fe tracks and Route 66 in Gallup.

The Fred Harvey Company in Kansas City, Missouri, in 1938 ordered six thousand color postcards showing the lobby at El Navajo. The card went into production at Curt Teich and Company on July 29, 1938, when employees assigned it stock number 8A-H1708 and Fred Harvey Company number H-3142. Staff artists retouched this black-and-white photograph to bring out details that they thought would enhance the quality of the postcard.

OK
Fred Harvey

5 3/16

5 1/8

(8)

H-3142   THE LOBBY, EL NAVAJO HOTEL, GALLUP, NEW MEXICO

H-4159 THE LOUNGE, LA POSADA, FRED HARVEY HOTEL, WINSLOW, ARIZONA

CHAPTER SEVEN

ARIZONA

JUST BEFORE THE LITTLE TOWN OF LUPTON, westbound travelers crossed into Arizona, arid country with giant red rocks and bluffs. The higher elevations trapped moisture, supporting pine trees, but within only a few miles the lower elevations were desert. These multiple grades proved to be demanding for many automobiles and trucks. For some the occasional steep ascents were too much, and the vehicles simply played out at the side of the road.

Arizona Route 66 travelers with sufficient means could find sumptuous lodgings at a series of hotels operated by the Fred Harvey Company alongside the tracks of the Atchison, Topeka and Santa Fe Railway, which roughly paralleled much of the highway. Among these lodgings were La Posada in Winslow, the Fray Marcos in Williams, the Escalante in Ash Fork, and the Havasu in Seligman. Other motorists could only imagine what it would be like to enjoy a hot bath and clean sheets. They might have only enough money for fuel and hopefully groceries, as they camped out on the ground beside their cars parked on the roadside. One step up was to patronize businesses like Kerby's Auto Camp in Seligman or Roy Walker's Free Camp Ground in Kingman. There one could usually park a car for free and pay to pitch a tent, take a cold shower, and buy basic foodstuffs.

Some tourists diverted northward from Highway 66 to drive about fifty miles to the rim of the Grand Canyon. Along their east–west route across Arizona, they also could drop off conveniently to the Painted Desert, the Petrified Forest, and the Meteor Crater.

At Peach Springs travelers passed through the heart of the Hualapai Indian reservation. There they could find fuel and groceries at the Peach Springs Trading Post, buy gasoline from Swedish immigrant John Osterman, or stay overnight in roadside cabins run by his brother, Oscar. The Santa Fe Railway for decades disputed with the tribe over ownership of the land beneath its rails; the Native people finally won a court case over the land in the 1940s. Farther along the road beyond Kingman, it climbed to 3,556 feet in elevation on a twisting, narrow way up Sitgreaves Pass before dropping back steeply down through Oatman to cross the Colorado River into California at Topock.

La Posada Hotel

WINSLOW, ARIZONA

1937

Among the Fred Harvey Company hotels that served as hubs for the Indian Detour sightseeing tours during the 1920s and 1930s, the westernmost was La Posada in Winslow, Arizona. It became the base for excursions by eastern and foreign tourists who arrived by Santa Fe trains and continued into the regions in special "Harveycar" motor coaches. There they visited such natural wonders as the Petrified Forest, the Painted Desert, and the Meteor Crater, as well as Hopi Indian villages.

Architect Mary Jane Colter, who started designing tourist facilities for the Fred Harvey Company in 1902, saw La Posada as her masterpiece. Although she was noted for helping to create the Pueblo Deco architectural style, Colter patterned the hotel in Winslow, its restaurant, and its depot more conservatively after an imaginary Spanish Colonial rancho of 150 years before. In her fantasy concept, the ranch property fell on hard times and was converted to a hotel but retained many of its old furnishings. The exterior and interior of the 1929 complex were designed to re-create in the guests' eyes such a former rancho. Thus the faux-adobe building received stucco finishes, flagstone floors, ceramic roof tiles, windows with shutters and iron grilles, and a sunken garden.

The south side of La Posada, seen in the photograph, had several brick platforms that facilitated the movement of passengers between trains and the combined hotel and station. The travelers passed on foot along a formal walkway through a landscaped open space from trackside to the main entry into the lodgings. In the picture a wisp of smoke from a steam locomotive wafts through the air. U.S. Highway 66 passed by on the far side of the complex.

The Fred Harvey Company in Kansas City, Missouri, submitted this black-and-white photograph with an order for six thousand color post-cards, requesting, "Show foliage around building as on photo att'd." The mailing reached Curt Teich and Company by February 22, 1937. On that day employees in Chicago gave the order stock number 7A-H647 and Fred Harvey Company number H-4220.

PHOTO BY TYNER-MURPHY KANSAS CITY, MO.

H-4224   LA POSADA, FRED HARVEY HOTEL, WINSLOW, ARIZONA

Passageway to West Wing, La Posada Hotel

WINSLOW, ARIZONA

1936

Architect Mary Jane Colter planned the interior arrangement of La Posada in an informal but carefully considered manner. It had two residential areas, with bedrooms and suites on the second floor of a central wing and rooms on both floors of a west wing. The photograph shows the corridor that linked the lobby with the west wing. At the east end of the building beyond the lobby were the dining room, coffee shop, bar, and newsstand. Covered walkways connected the lodgings with the train station, which lay closer to the tracks.

Construction on La Posada began in 1929, well before the October 29 stock market crash that began the Great Depression. Work continued on the effort, which was projected at $600,000 but ended up costing $1 million, and the hotel opened on 15 May 1930. Both the Santa Fe Railway and the Fred Harvey Company remained optimistic about the potential for tourism in the Southwest, even though railway passenger business had been diminishing year after year. Instead Americans increasingly took to the road in their own automobiles. Many of them preferred to camp at the roadside or stay in low-priced cabins rather than expensive hotels. Because of financial losses, the Harvey Company closed its restaurant in La Posada in 1956 and then the rest of the hotel in 1959.

The Santa Fe Railway converted the former hotel into offices. Partitions went up in the large open areas, and dropped ceilings obscured the wooden beams and painted ornamentation. The company auctioned off most of the custom furnishings that had helped make La Posada such an exceptional place to stay. At the end of her professional career, Mary Jane Colter reportedly declared, "Now I know there is such a thing as living too long." She died not long thereafter, believing that La Posada itself would eventually be torn down.

The Fred Harvey Company in Kansas City in 1936 requested six thousand color postcards from Curt Teich and Company showing the interior passageway to the west wing at La Posada. On May 29, 1936, a Teich employee assigned the printing job stock number 6A-H1029 and Fred Harvey Company number H-4157 and began the project.

82086

reprint 8½

H-4157   PASSAGEWAY TO WEST WING, LA POSADA, FRED HARVEY HOTEL, WINSLOW, ARIZONA

The Lounge, La Posada Hotel

WINSLOW, ARIZONA

1936

From the 1960s into the 1980s, the La Posada Hotel languished as an office building for employees of the Santa Fe Railway Company in Winslow. Because of its large number of transcontinental freight trains, the town was a logical place for the company to have divisional offices. Then the railroad moved out and in 1989 placed La Posada on its "disposal list." In 1992 local citizens gave the beloved landmark a measure of protection by successfully nominating it to the National Register of Historic Places. When the company in 1993 announced that it would cease maintaining the extensive grounds, local volunteers calling themselves the "gardening angels" took up the care, but everyone feared that the days of the grand old hotel were likely numbered.

La Posada needed a "guardian angel," and that came in the form of Allan Affeldt. After lengthy negotiations with the railroad company, in 1997 the preservationist from California purchased the eleven-acre La Posada complex and began a room-by-room restoration. The old hotel returned to limited operation that winter, and at the time of writing it had over fifty renovated rooms available to overnight guests. The old dining room was back in business as the chef-owned Turquoise Room Restaurant, offering memorable meals; some of the menu items came from the former Fred Harvey days.

The lounge in La Posada, shown in the photograph, was divided into multiple work spaces and meeting rooms during the two decades that the Santa Fe used the old hotel as an office building. The custom-made furnishings in the picture were all removed and mostly sold at auction, and the lovely ceilings were covered. The restoration of La Posada has returned the lounge area to its former uses, serving hotel guests as a casual setting for reading, amusing oneself at the piano, engaging in board games, and playing with children.

The Fred Harvey Company from Kansas City in 1936 sent a request to Curt Teich and Company for six thousand color postcards showing the lounge at La Posada. It reached the Chicago offices of the postcard company by May 29, 1936; on that day an employee assigned it stock number 6A-H1027 as well as Fred Harvey Company number H-4159.

H-4159   THE LOUNGE, LA POSADA, FRED HARVEY HOTEL, WINSLOW, ARIZONA

The Santa Fe *Super Chief*

NEAR FLAGSTAFF, ARIZONA

1937

The *Super Chief* train of the Atchison, Topeka and Santa Fe Railway was the first diesel-powered, all-sleeping-car passenger train in the United States. It ran between Chicago, Illinois, and Los Angeles, California, from 1936 to 1971, the end of Santa Fe passenger service. Throughout its operation, diesel locomotives drew the train, which consisted of air-conditioned sleeper cars, diner, and lounge. Widely known for its luxury and speed, the *Super Chief* became known in the 1930s and 1940s as the "Train of the Stars" for the Hollywood actors who frequently used it.

The Santa Fe had an important advantage over most of its competitors in transporting passengers between Chicago and Los Angeles: it owned all of the track over which its trains passed. One single operating department diverted slower-moving freight traffic out of the way for high-speed passenger trains to pass. This arrangement allowed the *Super Chief* to regularly make its entire trip between the two cities in less than forty hours. Initially the all-sleeper train ran once weekly in each direction and did not stop to board or disembark passengers at any stations between Kansas City and Barstow in Southern California. In this stretch it only made breaks to change crews or service the train. In 1948 daily operation began.

The photograph shows the *Super Chief* in 1936 or early 1937 on one of its four preview runs. These trips tested new snub-nosed diesel-electric locomotives that the General Motors Electro-Motive Corporation had designed and built for it in 1935. The photographer set up his camera on the U.S. Highway 66 overpass near Winona, Arizona, east of Flagstaff, to look down toward an S-curve in the Santa Fe double tracks. He snapped the shutter just as the eastbound train approached. Behind the double-unit locomotive we can see the heavyweight painted steel sleeping cars the *Super Chief* used until they were replaced by streamlined stainless steel sleepers in May 1937. Although the historic Route 66 overpass has been replaced, it is possible to view trains from a similar perspective from the current Arizona Highway 394 overpass across the tracks.

The Fred Harvey Company in Kansas City, Missouri, sent this photograph with an order for six thousand color postcards. The mailing reached Curt Teich and Company in Chicago by February 22, 1937, when employees began production by assigning it stock number 7A-H616. Then, for reasons not specified, production ceased. The company geographical index encompassing Arizona has a notation that this card was "never made up"—in other words, it was not ever printed.

Kaibab Motor Lodge

WILLIAMS, ARIZONA

1949

For seventy years the Kaibab Motor Lodge and its successors have sheltered travelers at the north side of historic U.S. Highway 66 on the extreme east side of Williams, Arizona. The town itself profited for decades from its location where the road (and later railroad) branched north to the Grand Canyon. It was the starting point for both the highway and a railroad spur that extended sixty miles north to the south rim of the Grand Canyon. Even in the days before trains and motor vehicles, travelers were funneled through Williams in stagecoaches and spring wagons to view the breathtaking gash in the earth. The geographically strategic position as gateway to the Grand Canyon, combined with other scenic attractions in the adjacent Kaibab National Forest, ensured tourist business for local entrepreneurs like the one who built the Kaibab Motor Lodge.

Oral traditions say that an unnamed veteran of the Depression-era Civilian Conservation Corps erected the initial buildings at the Kaibab Lodge about 1944. He had learned to work with concrete while helping to build a dam at Henderson, Nevada, and then applied those practical skills in Arizona. At the east side of Williams, he set up wooden forms and poured concrete to create the walls for an office and six cabins in a natural setting of a meadow and pines. The builder added gable roofs, steel casement windows, and furnishings, then opened for business. He consciously chose to locate his tourist court where it would be one of the first seen by westbound Route 66 motorists approaching the town. Over the years the Kaibab Motor Lodge expanded, adding more cabins, a swimming pool in 1959, and a railway caboose in the mid-1990s. At the time of writing, it was operating as the Canyon Motel and RV Park; much of its historic ambience has been preserved to enhance overnight stays by modern guests.

The Kaibab Motor Lodge ordered 12,500 color postcards from Curt Teich and Company in late summer 1949. The order, which received stock number 9B-H1145 in the Chicago offices on September 1, 1949, included this hand-tinted photograph with the instructions "Use tinted print as color guide."

KAIBAB MOTOR LODGE, WILLIAMS ARIZONA

KAIBAB MOTOR LODGE
WILLIAMS, ARIZONA

Havasu Hotel

SELIGMAN, ARIZONA

1952

The Fred Harvey Company operated its trackside hotels along the Santa Fe Railway across the American Southwest, but none of them was in a more out-of-the-way setting than the Havasu Hotel in Seligman, Arizona. However, the site happened to be in the right location for steam locomotives pulling trains to and from California to receive fuel and water while passengers took rest stops and ate meals. Katherine Krause Ferguson, the wife of a Harvey Company manager, remembered that when the hotel was built in 1905, there were so few business houses in Seligman that "you could look down Main Street and out to the desert."

The two-story Havasu Hotel took its name from the Indian tribe called Havasupai, a word that means "blue-green water." The two-story structure with a red tile roof and striking faux half-timbering housed the restaurant, hotel, and travelers' services. The National Old Trails Highway began bringing cross-country motorists to Seligman in 1912, and U.S. Highway 66 attracted more from 1926 onward. The existence of this luxury hotel offering fine meals in such a remote location must have seemed incongruous to many drivers. To attract patrons the Harvey Company erected a billboard three-quarters of a mile outside Seligman announcing to road-weary travelers that "Harvey House meals cost no more." The Havasu operated as a hotel and restaurant until 1954, when it became a railroad office building; it was demolished in 2008.

There were few visual distractions in Seligman, and it was also relatively close to Hollywood. The Havasu was thus a practical location choice for Metro-Goldwyn-Mayer Studios, which filmed its musical comedy motion picture *The Harvey Girls* there in 1945. This film, starring Judy Garland and Ray Bolger and released in 1946, is best known for a song from its score: "On the Atchison, Topeka and Santa Fe," by Henry Warren and Johnny Mercer. In the movie Judy Garland meets a group of young women headed by train to a mythical Arizona town to establish a Harvey House, joins them, experiences adventures, and eventually marries the handsome town saloonkeeper.

The Fred Harvey Company sent this photograph rubber stamped "1917" with an order for sixty-five hundred color postcards of the Havasu Hotel to Curt Teich and Company in early 1952. In Chicago printing house employees on February 22, 1952, assigned it stock number 2C-H338 and gave it Fred Harvey Company number H-5201.

SEP 24 1912

H-5201—The Havasu, Seligman, Arizona

Kerby's Auto Camp

SELIGMAN, ARIZONA

1926

Not all travelers through Seligman could afford the comfort the Fred Harvey Company provided at the Havasu Hotel. Others pinched their pennies to buy enough gasoline to reach their destinations. When nighttime dark overtook them and made further driving dangerous on yet-to-be-paved roadways, they pulled over to the roadside and pitched tents or slept in their cars. Those who could afford shelter might opt to stay in primitive cabins like those offered by Homer S. and Dora Kerby on the west side of the little Arizona town.

By the summer of 1926, the year the U.S. Bureau of Roads routed U.S. Highway 66 through Seligman, Mr. and Mrs. Kerby opened a combined garage, grocery store, and campground with cabins. The couple had come there after trying farming near Glendale in Maricopa County, Arizona, and their tenure on U.S. 66 in Seligman also proved to be short-lived. The roadside business showed up only in the 1927 annual volume of the *Arizona State Business Directory*; by 1929 the Kerbys were in Chandler, Arizona, city directories and Homer was identified as an automobile mechanic. By 1932 the telephone directory showed him as the proprietor of Kerby's Super Service Garage in Chandler, and by 1940 he had become owner of the H. S. Kerby Dodge-Plymouth automobile agency and was serving as a member of the Chandler city council. No references have been found for the Kerbys' brief enterprise in Seligman after the end of the 1920s.

Lodging offered in simple cabins along Route 66 in the Arizona desert was not necessarily up to the standards that travelers from the East expected. Unless they were fitted with crude evaporative air coolers, the quarters could be stiflingly hot during the summertime. In 1939 travel writer Janette Cooper Rutledge, who prided herself on the economy of the accommodations she used, advised, "Out on the desert pay close attention to how successfully the room has kept out desert pests."

On August 25, 1926, Curt Teich and Company received an order for one thousand postcards based on this photograph from distributor D. T. Mallonee in Phoenix, Arizona. He requested "blue sky" cards, which were printed in black-and-white but with light blue overprinted in the upper portion to simulate the hue of the heavens. Printing house employees assigned the card stock number 111076 and began preparing the materials for production.

KERBYS AUTO CAMP, WEST END, SELIGMAN, ARIZONA.   111076

85

Bird's-Eye View of Peach Springs

ARIZONA

1926

Peach Springs is known to southwesterners as the administrative center for the Hualapai Indian tribe in northwestern Arizona, but that distinction did not come until 1938, when the members formally voted to form a tribal council. During the late nineteenth and early twentieth centuries, it was known better to outsiders as a railroad town and division point on the Atchison, Topeka and Santa Fe Railway. Divisions were sections of track, often around a hundred miles long, that functioned as separate administrative units, and two of those segments came together at Peach Springs.

In 1866 the U.S. Congress chartered the Atlantic & Pacific Railroad to construct a transcontinental rail line that would cross Arizona. The company received land as a bonus for each mile of track laid. The Atlantic & Pacific laid its rails across Hualapai lands in 1883, the very same year that U.S. president Chester A. Arthur signed the executive decree recognizing the Hualapai Indian tribe. These events set up an inevitable dispute over land ownership. By the 1890s the Atchison, Topeka and Santa Fe Railway had acquired the old Atlantic & Pacific in stages and operated the rail line across Hualapai lands. The old land dispute between the railroad and the Hualapais continued into the 1940s, when the U.S. Supreme Court decided in favor of the Indians.

The railroad routed its tracks through Peach Springs for its known supply of clean water, suitable for steam locomotives. The company constructed large water-storage tanks, repair shops, supply yards for track maintenance, a depot, and even a Fred Harvey Company restaurant. Trains brought in supplies and merchandise and provided an outlet for cattle raised by the Hualapais. Thus a town populated by both Indians and whites grew up around the isolated railroad stop.

Postcard distributor D. T. Mallonee in Phoenix, Arizona, placed an order for one thousand black-and-white postcards showing a general view of Peach Springs and its railroad facilities for brothers John and Oscar Osterman to sell in their combined service station and garage at the town. The order reached Curt Teich and Company in Chicago by September 9, 1926, when printing house employees assigned the job stock number 111222 and put the card into production.

5 3/16 Square

BIRD'S EYE VIEW PEACH SPRINGS, ARIZONA ON OLD NATIONAL TRAILS HIGHWAY   111222

Main Street

PEACH SPRINGS, ARIZONA

1926

Remote Peach Springs unexpectedly received a connection to the outside world in addition to the one provided by the railroad. This link took the form of a coast-to-coast roadway. In the years before the numbering of highways, private organizations identified and signposted roads connecting cities. Among these groups was the National Old Trails Association, which organized itself in Kansas City in April 1912. It linked preexisting routes from New York City and Baltimore on the Atlantic with California on the Pacific, roughly following parts of two old wagon tracks, the old National Road in the east and the Santa Fe Trail in the west. Combining the titles provided the name, National Old Trails Highway. The mostly unpaved route included a dirt track parallel with the Santa Fe Railway across much of Arizona, including through Peach Springs.

The U.S. Bureau of Roads began assigning numbers to highways linking cities in multiple states during the mid-1920s, replacing the old regional naming system. Number 66 was assigned to the road between Chicago and Los Angeles, much of which followed the path already established by the National Old Trails Highway through Arizona and California. As increasing numbers of motorists came through Peach Springs on Route 66, enterprising businesspeople saw opportunities to open cafés, filling stations, garages, mercantile stores, and even auto campgrounds.

In July 1948 traveler Raymond G. Allen Jackson tarried for five days at Peach Springs, filling in for an Indian dishwasher in the Qumacho Café, one of its roadside businesses. The five regular pot-scrubbers, all Hualapai Indians, wanted time off to attend an Independence Day powwow, creating a need for short-term substitutes. During his stint as one of these temporary workers, Jackson saw how much effort was required to prepare and serve meals at the busy eatery in an out-of-the-way location. "This Peach Springs is an Indian reservation," Jackson noted, adding, "There are about five hundred of them." Of the Hualapai scullery workers, Jackson observed, "They make good help in the kitchen, although they . . . will not be rushed."

Distributor D. T. Mallonee in Phoenix, Arizona, enclosed this photograph of the Old National Trails Highway westbound through Peach Springs with a request for one thousand postcards showing the view. He placed the order on behalf of John and Oscar Osterman to sell in their garage and service station in the town. The two businessmen wanted "blue sky" postcards, which were printed in black and white but had light blue overprinting to simulate the appearance of the sky. The mailing reached Curt Teich and Company by September 9, 1926, the day the printing job received stock number 111219 and went into production.

MAIN ST., PEACH SPRINGS, ARIZONA, ON OLD NATIONAL TRAILS HIGHWAY.   111219

87

Peach Springs Trading Post

PEACH SPRINGS, ARIZONA

1928

From the 1920s to the 1970s, the Peach Springs Trading Post served as a major mercantile outlet in the little town in the Hualapai Indian Reservation of northwestern Arizona. Not only did the store sell food, hardware, and general household goods; it also marketed arts and crafts made by Hualapais and other Indians in the region. It was perhaps the most important of the places where now-sought-after antique Hualapai baskets were originally sold.

E. H. Carpenter established the trading post at Peach Springs as a general mercantile store in a wood-frame building in 1917. In 1921 he took in Ancel L. Taylor as a partner. Seeing opportunities in the growing road traffic through the town, Taylor bought Carpenter out and became the sole owner of the business in 1924. In 1928 he replaced the old wooden building with the new stone structure seen in the picture.

Understanding the requirements of managing a store as a white man on an Indian reservation, Ancel Taylor secured a government license, posted a liability bond, and accepted traditional Hualapai crafts and locally raised beef in exchange for packaged foods, cloth, medicines, tobacco, hardware, and kerosene. He also catered to the needs of motorists driving on U.S. Highway 66 by handling gasoline, oil, and other automotive supplies. Victor and Grace Bracke purchased the Peach Springs Trading Post in 1936 and managed the business much as their predecessors had. About 1950 the Hualapai Tribe acquired the trading post, operating it as a general mercantile store into the early 1970s, when it erected a new grocery outlet. After that time other tribal entities used the building, which was placed on the National Register of Historic Places in 2003.

During the summer of 1928, distributor D. T. Mallonee of Phoenix, Arizona, placed an order for one thousand "blue sky" postcards showing part of the newly erected masonry Peach Springs Trading Post. In the view a motorist was filling an automobile with gasoline at the side of U.S. Highway 66. A big sign above advertising the availability of ladies' restrooms was decorated with swastikas, a traditional American Indian symbol. The order and photograph reached Curt Teich and Company in Chicago by July 20, 1928, when it was assigned stock number 121906 and production began.

PEACH SPRINGS TRADING POST, PEACH SPRINGS, ARIZONA

88

O. C. Osterman Auto Court

PEACH SPRINGS, ARIZONA

1934

Two brothers from Sweden made their home in Mojave County, Arizona, during the early twentieth century, leaving their mark on the history of Peach Springs. The first to arrive was John Osterman, who as a sailor jumped ship on the coast of Mexico and made his way into Arizona about 1914. He worked for a while at a dairy in Phoenix, Arizona, and then on a ranch near Peach Springs. In 1923, after returning from U.S. military service during World War I, Osterman opened a service station on the National Old Trails Highway in Peach Springs. He erected a concrete block replacement in 1929, and that structure, listed on the National Register of Historic Places, still stood on the south side of the highway in the village at the time of writing.

With increased motor traffic following the designation of the road through Peach Springs as U.S. Highway 66 in 1926, John Osterman recognized the expanding economic opportunities and invited his brother, Oscar C., to join him in Arizona. Oscar erected a handful of wooden cabins next door to his brother's service station about 1932. He reputedly rented them for a dollar a night and made back his initial investment during the first summer. Next he constructed a row of fourteen tourist-court units, an office, and bathhouse.

By 1938 Frank and Beatrice Boyd had purchased the facility, renaming it the Peach Springs Auto Court. The couple operated the lodging until Frank's death, and Beatrice continued managing the motel into the early 1980s. Subsequently all the buildings were removed from the site, part of which was later occupied by modern construction of the Hualapai Lodge operated by the Hualapai Tribe.

The Peach Springs Garage ordered one thousand black-and-white postcards based on this photograph showing the O. C. Osterman Auto Court. The materials reached Curt Teich and Company in Chicago by May 24, 1934; on that date employees assigned the job stock number D-3445 and began the printing process.

O. C. OSTERMAN AUTO COURT — PEACH SPRINGS, ARIZONA — U.S. ROUTE 66

Roy's Free Camp Ground and Service Station

KINGMAN, ARIZONA

1926

The Kingman, Arizona, area was tied to transportation even before the town was founded. In 1857 an expedition of army engineers headed by Lieutenant Edward F. Beale passed through its valley between the Cerbat and Hualapai mountain ranges, surveying the path for a wagon road that later became part of the route for the Atlantic & Pacific Railroad across Arizona. The arrival of steel rails in 1882 ensured prosperity for what became the town of Kingman, making it an outbound shipping point for minerals and cattle and an inbound destination for people and goods. The later development of overland roads and then highways only enhanced Kingman's strategic importance.

Starting in 1912 the National Old Trails Highway funneled motorists through Kingman, and even more started arriving in 1926, when the way was designated as U.S. Highway 66. Many businesspeople in the community gravitated to the unpaved east–west road parallel with the railroad tracks, providing travelers with fuel, food, and shelter.

One of these businesspeople was Ohio-born Roy Walker, who as early as the mid-1920s operated a combined filing station, secondhand store, and campground alongside the highway. He continued selling previously owned merchandise through the 1930s, while at the same time dabbling in real estate. Walker eventually became a broker, with an office at 243–45 East Beale Street. He and his wife, Georgia, by the 1940s also operated a Texaco service station and adjacent café on the east side of town. Not everything went well for Roy Walker, however. In circumstances not fully understood, on May 21, 1950, at age sixty-five he took his own life in the alley behind a drugstore in Kingman; his mortal remains were interred in the local Mountain View Cemetery.

On August 4, 1926, Curt Teich and Company in Chicago received an order for one thousand "blue sky" postcards for Roy's Free Camp Ground and Service Station in Kingman. These were cards printed in black-and-white but overprinted with light blue to simulate the appearance of the sky. Teich employees gave the printing job stock number 110889 and started the project.

ROY'S FREE CAMP GROUND AND SERVICE STATION, KINGMAN, ARIZONA.

110889

City Café and Texaco Station

KINGMAN, ARIZONA

1951

For decades the City Café and its adjacent Texaco service station were landmarks for travelers driving through Kingman, Arizona, on U.S. Highway 66. According to files at the local Mohave Museum of History and Arts, local real estate broker Roy Walker was the key figure in constructing the City Café between 1939 and 1942. The eatery fronted on the northwest side of U.S. Highway 66 in its 1900 block at the east side of the town. The Texaco service station, housed in its own standard-plan, enamel-veneer building, also opened about 1939. Over the years it and the café became institutions in the Arizona town.

Although Kingman already had considerable traffic in the 1930s, it still was not an easy place to find a good meal. This situation presented Roy Walker with the opportunity to establish the City Café. Four years before the café opened, in 1935, British traveler Mark Pepys had driven through and reported, "Feeding at Kingman was a primitive business." He and a companion walked into a café housed in a narrow commercial building fronting on the highway. "We chose a table next to the curtained window and ordered what seemed safest: thin soup and part of a freshly killed fowl." The decision was only satisfactory at best, as the visitor declared, "The bird proved to be without doubt the oldest inhabitant." Even cleaning up before the meal proved to be difficult, as there was no place to wash one's hands. Pepys narrated, "I explored the kitchen where the cook, a large man, slow and amiable of speech, filled a tin basin with hot water for me."

The City Café answered the dining needs of Route 66 motorists for almost seventy years. A 1956 road travel guide described it as "a very good air cond[itioned] café serving food at reasonable prices. . . . Open 24 hours." Through a succession of proprietors, the eatery lost its front parking area to widening of the highway and then most of its east-side parking through the creation of Stockton Hill Road. Leaks in the flat roof of the Art Deco masonry building prompted one of the later owners to add an incongruous separate gable roof, but the diner kept serving meals. In 2005 new owners changed its name to Hot Rod Café, and then in 2009 the café and the entire block to the west, including the service station, were removed to make way for a new Walgreen's drugstore.

On June 20, 1951, Curt Teich and Company received an order for 12,500 color postcards of the City Café and Texaco Station from the Earl J. Brothers Desert Souvenir Supply Company in Boulder City, Nevada. Printing house staff in Chicago gave the job stock number 1C-H852 and began production.

204

City Cafe and Texaco Station, Kingman, Arizona

Colorado River Bridge

TOPOCK, ARIZONA

1927

Erected in 1916, the Colorado River Bridge, known also as the Old Trails Bridge, was only the second permanent highway bridge constructed across the Colorado River to link Arizona with California.

The route across the United States of the National Old Trails Highway initially took it across the Colorado River by ferry at Topock, Arizona. The ferry and landings were swept away by a massive flood in 1914. After this inundation motorists were forced either to drive precariously balanced on wooden timbers positioned outside the rails on a nearby Santa Fe Railway bridge or to detour 185 miles south via unpaved roads to cross the river on the one auto bridge at Yuma. In light of these problems, the states of Arizona and California joined with the U.S. Bureau of Indian Affairs to pool funding and erect a highway bridge at Topock.

The handsome new bridge consisted of a steel arch 592 feet long and had a total length of 832 feet, making it the longest steel arch bridge in the United States on its completion. The 360-ton structure also held the distinction of being the lightest and longest three-hinged steel arch in the country. The Colorado River Bridge carried the National Old Trails Highway and then U.S. Highway 66 across the Colorado River from its dedication on March 25, 1916, until 1947. This is the steel arch bridge over which the Joad family drove into California in the 1940 John Ford movie *The Grapes of Wrath*. After it ceased to transport motor vehicles, the Colorado River Bridge was adapted to carry a natural gas pipeline for the Pacific Gas and Electric Company, a role it continued to play at the time of writing.

Postcard distributor D. T. Mallonee in Phoenix, Arizona, in late spring 1927 ordered one thousand black-and-white postcards illustrating the Colorado River Bridge on behalf of the Topock Camp in Topock. The request reached Curt Teich and Company in Chicago by June 2, 1927, the day Teich employees assigned it stock number 114826 and began production.

COLORADO RIVER BRIDGE. TOPOCK. ARIZONA

114826

THIRD STREET, LOOKING EAST, SAN BERNARDINO, CALIFORNIA

122323

CALIFORNIA

ROUTE 66 MOTORISTS CROSSED THE COLORADO RIVER into California from Arizona on a 1916 steel arch bridge. The miles ahead through the Mojave Desert must have tried the patience of those who thought the Golden State would immediately be the land of milk and honey. This stretch of the 66 Highway was the most taxing on both humans and motor vehicles. Summertime temperatures generally reached 120 degrees and higher. The worst stretches of desert were between Needles and Victorville, after which the aridity gradually moderated.

After crossing the Cajon Summit between the San Bernardino and the San Gabriel Mountains beyond Victorville, drivers gradually descended into the California that they knew from tourist brochures and Hollywood films. Beyond San Bernardino came seemingly endless orange groves and roadways lined with picturesque eucalyptus trees. After the extremes of the Mojave, places like Monrovia and Pasadena must have seemed like paradise.

Los Angeles itself was the magnet for many of the Highway 66 travelers. The metropolis offered visitors choices among Hollywood performers at Earl Carroll's Theater Restaurant; exotic dishes at Clifton's Pacific Seas Cafeteria, which had an artificial waterfall on its front; and meals over the ocean at O. J. Bennett's Sea Food Grotto.

The highway continued to its traditional end in Santa Monica at the Pacific Ocean, at the juncture of Santa Monica Boulevard and Ocean Avenue. There visitors often made their way to a 1952 memorial to Oklahoma-born humorist Will Rogers, who died in a plane crash in 1935. In his honor road promoters had given U.S. 66 the additional name of Will Rogers Highway. Motorists who made "the California trip" to Santa Monica could frolic in the waters of the Pacific or simply sit back on park benches and reflect on their successful sojourn crossing the nation along the Mother Road.

Front Street

NEEDLES, CALIFORNIA

1927

Needles, California, owed its existence and long-term prosperity to transportation. Located at a village of indigenous Mojave Indians, it became a mid-nineteenth-century steamboat landing on the banks of the Colorado River. Then in 1883 tracks laid by the Southern Pacific Railway arrived from the west, while the Atlantic & Pacific Railroad (later Santa Fe Railway) laid its track to the opposite bank of the Colorado River. Before completion of a truly permanent bridge across the river seven years later, Needles boomed as a place of interchange between waterborne and rail freight.

The two railway lines carried manufactured goods to Needles, which became a distribution point for much of the Mojave Desert country. The rail lines likewise opened access to ores extracted in mining communities on both sides of the Colorado River, contributing to the town's growth. In time dams on the Colorado River blocked steamboat traffic, but by then the National Old Trails Highway and later U.S. Highway 66 were bringing more and more motorists through Needles, especially after completion of the steel arch highway bridge across the Colorado in 1916.

The commercial buildings that faced the 700 block of Front Street, opposite from the railway yards in Needles, bespoke the prosperity of the downtown area. Structures as tall as four stories graced the broad way. At the end of the street, on the right, a grove of trees shaded Santa Fe Park, which sat beside a handsome Fred Harvey hotel. Today this district has been transformed, again by the forces of transportation. All of the commercial buildings seen in this picture of the 700 block in Front Street have been removed and replaced with paving, enabling trucks and motor vehicles access to modern commercial businesses on the opposite side of the block.

Distributor D. T. Mallonee in Phoenix, Arizona, ordered one thousand black-and-white postcards based on this retouched photographic street scene in Needles. The packet of materials reached Curt Teich and Company by June 13, 1927, when its employees gave the job stock number 115013 and began production.

FRONT STREET, NEEDLES, CALIFORNIA.   115013

El Garces Hotel

NEEDLES, CALIFORNIA

1927

As part of its network of hotels and eating houses serving travelers on the Atchison, Topeka and Santa Fe Railway, the Fred Harvey Company operated El Garces Hotel in Needles from the facility's opening in 1908 until its closure in 1949. Named in honor of 1770s southwestern explorer Father Francisco Garcés, the ornate concrete structure has been identified as the most significant Classical Revival railway depot in California. It fronted directly on the National Old Trails Highway and the initial alignment of U.S. Highway 66.

In the 1880s Needles was one of the major operational centers on the Santa Fe Railway line connecting Southern California with the rest of the nation. Dozens of trains passed through the town daily to and from the nearby bridge crossing the Colorado River. Because the Santa Fe during its early days did not provide rolling dining cars for its passengers, these travelers needed places to eat while the trains paused at trackside. An earlier station and eating house at Needles burned in 1906, so the railway company filled the gap by erecting a massive, 518-foot-long two-story combined station, restaurant, and hotel complex fronting on the tracks. Taking ideas from classical Greece and Rome, architect Francis Wilson designed the building with multicolumned loggias and porticos. It served the public until 1949, when the facility was converted to house Santa Fe Railway offices for another four decades. After substantial renovations, the building reopened in 2014 as the community intermodal transportation center.

Even though Needles, on the edge of the Mojave Desert, typically endured summertime high temperatures around 120 degrees Fahrenheit, many people viewed El Garces as the pinnacle of the Fred Harvey Company's service and luxury. Employees vied for positions in the prestigious location. On October 27, 1922, motorist Vernon McGill stayed at El Garces and described the "artistic beauty" he beheld "through the French doors which open on to . . . immense tropical palms, ten to fifteen feet high, gently waving in the hotel grounds." But not every overnight guest found things quite so charming. In 1930 Hoffman Birney complained of getting no sleep in his room: "There was a hole in the screen. The Colorado River mosquitoes found the hole first and while one stood outside and rang the dinner bell his little playmates piled through and held high revel on my unclad carcass."

Postcard distributor D. T. Mallonee in Phoenix, Arizona, placed an order for one thousand black-and-white postcards based on this photograph of El Garces as seen from the east, showing multiple parallel tracks and platforms in the foreground. The request reached Curt Teich and Company by June 13, 1927; that day printing house employees assigned it stock number 115014 and started production.

HARVEY HOUSE, NEEDLES, CALIFORNIA.

Bender's One Stop Super Service Station

AMBOY, CALIFORNIA

1932

In 1883 the Southern Pacific Railroad created a siding named Amboy in the Mojave Desert. Wells drilled there struck only salt water, so the company hauled locomotive boiler water in tank cars from Newberry Springs to the west. A small town grew up around the siding. Then in 1912 the National Old Trails Highway was routed through the track-side community, followed by U.S. Highway 66 in 1926. The additional road traffic brought more trade to the tiny community, prompting several entrepreneurs to open filling stations, simple stores, garages, and tourist cabins.

Ben Benjamin is credited with establishing Amboy's first filling station and store catering specifically to motorists. He owned property on both sides of the highway, and in the mid-1920s he sold tracts on the north side to Roy Crowl and Bill Lee. Benjamin then used the proceeds from the land sales to erect his own Standard Oil Company station at the west end of the village. This north-facing location permitted the awning on the front of his station to create welcome shade from the desert sun. Not long thereafter Crowl and Lee constructed their own competing enterprises on the other side of the road; at the time of writing, the former's effort survived as Roy's Café and Motel.

Benjamin sold his business to German-born Joseph M. Bender, who in the 1920 census was listed as running a store just to the west at Bagdad,

Amboy Calif.

California. His brother Martin "Mart" joined him in Amboy; the two of them were recorded there in the 1930 census, Joe running the combined station and store and Martin serving as the postmaster inside. By 1932 they had erected a row of simple wooden cottages to house some of their employees and motorists seeking lodging. They called the complex Bender's One Stop Super Service.

In 1948 the Bender family sold the business to Constantine "Conn" and Lillie Pulos, and it went through various other hands until it closed in 1973, the year the old 66 Highway through Amboy was bypassed by Interstate 40. At the time of writing, only a few concrete footings and driveways survived from Bender's former business on the south side of the road.

During the summer of 1932, Bender's One Stop Super Service ordered six thousand composite black-and-white postcards showing the cabins at their filling station in Amboy. Curt Teich and Company employees received the packet with the original photographs by June 13, 1932, and assigned the printing job stock number D-2232.

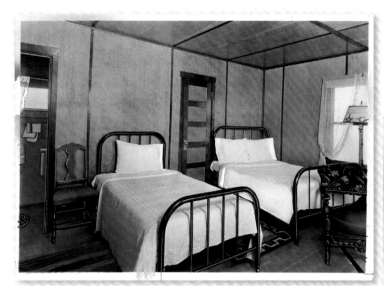

2½ Square

BENDER'S ONE STOP SUPER SERVICE STATION

INTERIOR OF COTTAGE

PORTION OF LOBBY

COMFORT ON THE DESERT   *Air Conditioned*   AMBOY, CALIF.

D-2232

Southwest on Main Street

1927

Travel writer Jack D. Rittenhouse in 1946 characterized Ludlow as "a real town in comparison to the one-establishment places passed on the way here from Needles." He was right: the Mojave Desert community was one of the few places on the road between Needles and Barstow that was large enough to be viewed as a township. It came into existence in 1883, when the Southern Pacific Railroad placed a siding there while laying its rails. The next year the Santa Fe Railway acquired the line, which brought people, goods, and income to the otherwise isolated desert locality. Construction in 1905 of the 169-mile Tonopah and Tidewater Railroad, which ran northward from Ludlow to the mining boomtowns of Tonopah, Rhyolite, and Beatty in Nevada, assured prosperity for merchants at the junction, as did a line eight miles south to the Buckeye Mining District.

The National Old Trails Road was routed through Ludlow in 1912, and U.S. Highway 66 followed in 1926, ensuring that motorists would bring their own trade to the Mojave Desert community. Consequently impresarios who were already supplying mines and miners opened additional filling stations, garages, eating places, hotels, and campgrounds to cater to customers arriving by automobile. Highway traffic passed through the town until 1973, when it was bypassed by Interstate 40.

The photographer pointed his camera southwestward on Main Street to take the photograph along U.S. Highway 66, excluding from the view the railroad tracks just to the left. Toward the far end of the street on the right, at the Murphy Bro. Café sign, the two-story concrete Ludlow Mercantile Company building still stands. Thomas and Michael Murphy owned this emporium, which offered hotel rooms upstairs. The *Barstow Printer* newspaper published a brief report about the store in 1922: "Here a free campground has been built and baths put in for the convenience of travelers." The journalist lauded local residents for keeping their city tidy, stating, "The absence of tin cans and rubbish piles along the approaches to the town are appreciated."

Phoenix, Arizona, postcard distributor D. T. Mallonee placed an order for one thousand black-and-white cards of this Ludlow street scene. His materials reached Curt Teich and Company by November 27, 1927, when employees in Chicago assigned the job stock number 117668 and began the printing process.

MAIN STREET. LUDLOW. CALIFORNIA.

117668

Northeast on Main Street

LUDLOW, CALIFORNIA

1927

While the store and café of Murphy Brothers greeted 1920s motorists arriving in Ludlow from the southwest, competing enterprises owned by George E. and Lena E. Reed met those entering town from the northeast. Their businesses included the Oasis Hotel, the Oasis Garage, the Oasis Free Campgrounds, and the Oasis Café. As if this were not enough to absorb their energies, Mrs. Reed also served as the longtime Ludlow postmaster. In the middle of the Reeds' multiple establishments, the Murphy Brothers ran their garage, which doubled as the local Ford automobile dealership.

Garages were essential in Ludlow, for the mechanical demands of driving across the Mojave Desert took a heavy toll on vehicles. Motorist Dallas Lore Sharp in 1928, the year after this picture was taken, wrote this vivid description of what he observed while motoring across the barren wastes along U.S. Highway 66: "From Needles on to Barstow a line of motor wreckage had strewn our shore. Dismembered parts of automobiles made the prospect grewsome [sic]. Blistered, blown-out, disemboweled tires told an awful story of . . . the eviscerating lava rock in the road." His chronicle continued in that key: "Unhallowed as junk, protruding from the drifting sand, or prone where they had fallen, lay the bones of every known species of car."

For travelers crossing mile after mile in such desolation, Ludlow was indeed a haven. It was no accident that Mr. and Mrs. George E. Reed chose to use the word "oasis" to name each of the businesses they operated. A writer for the *Barstow Printer* described the gardenlike appearance the town presented to visitors in 1922: "The trees and shrubbery attract attention and show that the residents take an interest in making their place attractive. And then when the traveler learns that the water for irrigation and also for drinking purposes is hauled 30 miles [by railway tank car], he certainly admires the pluck of Ludlow residents."

Postcard distributor D. T. Mallonee in Phoenix, Arizona, placed an order for one thousand black-and-white cards depicting this view of Ludlow. His materials made their way to Curt Teich and Company in Chicago by November 17, 1927, and staff there assigned the printing order stock number 117667.

MAIN STREET, LUDLOW, CALIFORNIA.

117667

Desert Inn Hotel

Throughout the Desert Southwest, Chinese-born immigrants found opportunities to operate businesses on their own and to build successful careers. One of these was Yim Lee, who for years ran the Desert Inn at Ludlow. Downstairs in the wood-frame building, Lee offered hot and cold meals plus ice cream and cold carbonated drinks. On the side he sold sundry tobacco products and sweets. A 1922 article in the *Barstow Printer* reported, "Lee . . . is conducting the 'Desert Inn' and advertising 'meals at sensible prices.' . . . [He] is assisted in waiting on his trade by his wife and two children."

Yim Lee was just one member of a larger family serving motorists in the Mojave Desert. One of his cousins was Bill Lee, who purchased property on the north side of U.S. Highway 66 in Amboy from Ben Benjamin and erected a café and then a well-patronized Texaco service station. Lee's business predated that of his next-door neighbor, Roy Crowl, who in 1938 opened the still-surviving Roy's Motel and Café. One more entrepreneur in the Lee family was Chester Lee in Saltus, just southeast of Amboy.

Another notable Chinese businessman who also served 1920s motorists on Route 66 in the Mojave Desert was Gee King. He not only ran the Oasis Café in Ludlow for Mr. and Mrs. George E. Reed, but also owned an eating house that served travelers in nearby Bagdad, California.

In 1926, the year the U.S. Bureau of Roads assigned number 66 to the highway connecting Chicago with Los Angeles, postcard distributor D. T. Mallonee in Phoenix, Arizona, ordered a thousand black-and-white cards showing the Desert Inn Hotel that fronted on the roadway in Ludlow. The photograph and other materials reached Curt Teich and Company in Chicago by December 6, 1926, when employees there gave the job stock number 112576 and began preparing it for publication.

DESERT INN HOTEL, LUDLOW, CALIF.

112574

221

Street Scene

VICTORVILLE, CALIFORNIA

1927

"You leave the desert behind at Victorville," wrote westbound Route 66 traveler Hoffman Birney in 1930. His description of the landscape change was apt: the town was indeed where motorists left behind the bare earth and scattered cactus of the wasteland only five hundred feet above sea level and climbed three thousand feet, to a visibly different natural vegetation typified by Joshua trees and yuccas. After travelers had passed through oppressive summertime heat in the desert, they entered at Victorville an environment with "one of the healthiest climates," according to a 1949 Shell Oil Company tourist guide, thanks to its "light, dry, pure air."

From 1926 to 1972 U.S. Highway 66 traversed the heart of Victorville. Los Angeles–bound drivers entered the town from the northwest, crossing the Mojave River, and then turned southwest to continue the ascent toward the Cajon Summit crossing between the San Bernardino and the San Gabriel Mountains. The photograph was made looking northwestward and shows the right-angle intersection where motorists swung from northwest–southeast D Street onto southwest–northeast Seventh Street at the edge of what used to be the main commercial district.

The two-story brick commercial structure on the left in the photograph was the early twentieth-century Vandiver Building. Over the years it housed multiple businesses catering to both travelers and locals, including the Stewart Hotel, the Victor Valley Mercantile, the Paragon Market, and even the local post office. A sign mounted on a utility pole points one block southwest on Seventh toward the Oasis Café, a prominent eatery that served many Route 66 drivers and later relocated to the Vandiver Building as well. As early as 1916 the local press declared, "The Oasis has a splendid reputation among the traveling public, and auto tourists say they cannot find anything which equals it." The entire area depicted in the 1927 image has changed drastically over the years: trees have been cut down, and the Vandiver Building site, at the time of writing, was occupied by a modern gas station–convenience store.

Postcard distributor D. T. Mallonee in Phoenix, Arizona, ordered one thousand "blue sky" postcards based on this photograph for newspaperman Walker Jones in Victorville, California. The request reached Curt Teich and Company in Chicago by February 21, 1927, the date an employee rubber stamped its paperwork after the printing job had been assigned stock number 113356.

STREET SCENE, VICTORVILLE, CALIFORNIA

113356

Third Street

SAN BERNARDINO,

CALIFORNIA

1928

When a photographer stepped out onto West Third Street in downtown San Bernardino to snap this east-facing picture of its intersection with North E Street in 1928, the city was booming. Located in an area of productive agriculture and straddling important rail and highway links with the rest of the nation, it boasted about forty-two thousand people and a thriving commercial district. The constant movement of traffic on U.S. Highway 66, which skirted downtown but still flowed right through the community, brought decades of steady income.

The picture recorded the commercial center of San Bernardino during the time of perhaps its greatest prosperity. On the right side stood the newly erected 1927 Harris Building (with an ornate arched entry), which had grown from a small dry goods concern in 1905 into a palatial four-story department store. Beyond the juncture with North E Street, the 1890s Stewart Hotel provided downtown lodging for commercial and other travelers until it burned in 1935.

Nearest to the photographer on the left side was F. W. Woolworth's variety store, and the Chocolate Palace Café and a sporting goods store shared the next two spaces. At the corner stood the five-story 1927 Andreson Building, for years home to the Merchants Bank and later the Bank of America. Just on the other side of the intersection stood the turn-of-the-twentieth-century Katz Building, which housed dry goods sales, drugstores, retail outlets, and offices.

After World War II the suburbs of San Bernardino continued to grow, but the city as a whole wobbled into economic doldrums. Several of its larger employers closed, while nearby Riverside and Ontario supplanted the older city as an economic center for the east end of the Los Angeles metropolitan area. In an effort to revive its stagnant central core, the local government secured grants that partially funded removal of many substandard buildings and the creation of the 1972 Central City Mall, which absorbed about a dozen square blocks of former downtown buildings. Attached to the complex, the old Harris Department Store became one of the three retail sales anchors for the massive project. The Andreson Building was just far enough away to avoid being gobbled up as well. The project never profited as expected, even when reconfigured into the Carousel Mall. At the time of writing, the failed downtown development scheme faced possible deconstruction.

The San Bernardino F. W. Woolworth store, shown at the left edge of the photograph, ordered thirty-five hundred color postcards of this view on Third Street. Its materials reached Curt Teich and Company in Chicago by August 17, 1928, the day printers assigned it stock number 122323 and started production.

THIRD STREET, LOOKING EAST, SAN BERNARDINO, CALIFORNIA   122323

Leven Oaks Hotel

MONROVIA, CALIFORNIA

1927

After westbound motorists on Route 66 had driven through the desolate Mojave Desert, they began entering towns that offered more temperate climate and vegetation. Passing through and then along the wooded San Gabriel Mountains, new arrivals came to Monrovia. They knew that they had reached "civilization" when they found well-established luxury lodgings at the Leven Oaks Hotel.

One of the founders of Monrovia, John D. Bicknell, decided in 1911 that the community would benefit from a first-class hotel. His goal was to attract seasonal residents from the northern states to "winter" in temperate California. He purchased a tract of land on South Myrtle Avenue that already had a grove of oak trees. He hired architects to design a public lodging organized like Swiss hotels but in the popular Spanish Renaissance Revival style, leaving as many trees undisturbed as possible. These trees gave the hotel its name.

Leven Oaks opened on December 11, 1911—over five hundred people attended the ceremonies—and operated at 120 South Myrtle Avenue near the downtown commercial district for many years. This location was only half a block south of West Foothill Boulevard, which in time carried U.S. Highway 66 traffic through the town. Over the years many Route 66 travelers lodged there. As tastes in overnight accommodations changed, the Leven Oaks declined in the second half of the twentieth century. Then it came back to life in 1984 as an assisted-living facility; at the time of writing it continued to serve that role.

The Leven Oaks Hotel in Monrovia sent this photograph to Curt Teich and Company with a request for six thousand color postcards. The packet of materials reached the printing house by November 27, 1927, two days after Thanksgiving. There an employee assigned the job stock number 117903 and made a notation, "It will be necessary to cut 1" off at the top and 1" at the bottom, in order to get the right proportion."

LEVEN OAKS HOTEL, MONROVIA, CALIFORNIA.

117903

101

Francois French Restaurant

PASADENA, CALIFORNIA

1938

When westbound motorists on Route 66 topped the pass at the Cajon Summit and began dropping down into the San Gabriel Valley, the landscape began changing from semiarid scrub brush to orange groves, eucalyptus trees, and a series of inviting towns. Pasadena was perhaps the most appealing town in this string of communities, as it had developed since the 1880s as a winter resort for wealthy easterners. As early as 1890 its municipal leaders hosted an annual New Year's Day Tournament of Roses parade to "tell the world about our paradise."

In Pasadena travelers not only obtained comfortable lodgings, but also found restaurants offering some of the best meals they had encountered since leaving the Mississippi Valley. The Francois French Restaurant clearly represented this higher class of dining establishments where customers enjoyed delicious fare.

Emile Poupon and Francois Giacomone about 1932 established the Emile and Francois Restaurant in a building fronting onto U.S. Highway 66 located in the old commercial district of Pasadena at 46 East Colorado Boulevard. Poupon departed the business within a few months, but his partner continued to operate it as the Francois Giacomone Restaurant. The bistro featured French country food: diners shared family-style bowls of salad and tureens of soup. The slogan the restaurant used in advertising was *Un repas sans vin est une journée sans soleil,* "A meal without wine is a day without sunshine." Such Los Angeles–based organizations as the France-Amériques Club made it a regular meeting place. Pasadena city directories indicate that the location expanded to 44–46 East Colorado Boulevard by 1936 and became 44 East Colorado by 1939. This favorite restaurant served the public through World War II but closed by the time the first postwar city directory was issued in 1947.

On November 25, 1938, Curt Teich and Company received an order from the Francois French Restaurant two thousand black-and-white postcards based on this interior photograph. Employees in Chicago began the printing job by assigning it stock number D-5661.

FRANCOIS FRENCH RESTAURANT   46 E Colorado St. PASADENA. CALIFORNIA

UN REPAS SANS VIN EST UNE JOURNEE SANS SOLEIL

FRANCOIS FRENCH RESTAURANT — PASADENA, CALIFORNIA

102

Arroyo Seco Parkway

LOS ANGELES, CALIFORNIA

1941

The Arroyo Seco Parkway holds the distinctions of being the first freeway constructed west of the Mississippi River and a prototype for freeways built in many parts of the United States. When the roadway opened in 1941, it became the official route of U.S. Highway 66 between Pasadena and Los Angeles; the earlier Figueroa Street alignment became Alternate U.S. 66.

The freeway took its name from the Spanish term *arroyo seco*, meaning "dry gulch." An intermittent stream by that name carried occasional storm flows from the San Gabriel Mountains down to the Los Angeles River in central Los Angeles, and much of the road construction followed the west bank of that watercourse.

Freeways generally are defined as thoroughfares with divided lanes for traffic, high-speed movement, and limited access from side roads. Designers incorporated all of these elements into the Arroyo Seco Parkway. In addition, they created a thoroughfare patterned after scenic parkways elsewhere in the country, blending landscaping of native plants and trees with the safety features needed for high-speed travel. Construction began in 1938 and continued by stages, and the completed freeway was formally dedicated on January 30, 1941.

Engineers designed the freeway with two 11- to 12-foot-wide driving lanes and one 10-foot shoulder in each direction. The outer two lanes were paved with Portland cement, while the inner passing lanes were covered in black asphalt. As traffic flow increased, the shoulders were converted to driving lanes as well, and the speed limit increased from forty-five to fifty-five miles per hour. At the time of writing, the roadway remained fully operational as the Pasadena Freeway / California State Highway 101.

The Western Publishing and Novelty Company in Los Angeles placed an order for twenty-five thousand color postcards based on this photograph of the Arroyo Seco Parkway; its materials reached the publisher in Chicago by October 29, 1941. Printing house staff gave it stock number 1B-H2162 and noted that the card should also be imprinted with private number LA-121.

LA-121—Arroyo-Seco Parkway, Los Angeles-Pasadena, California

U. S. Highway 66

1B-H2162

Clifton's Pacific Seas Cafeteria

LOS ANGELES, CALIFORNIA

1946

From the 1930s onward Clifton's Cafeterias were culinary landmarks in Los Angeles. The first of the Clifton's downtown eateries, at 618 South Olive Street, became a visual landmark as well. In 1939 its building was completely renovated to simulate a South Seas island paradise, complete with tropical plants, vines, and even a real flowing waterfall on its front above the sidewalk.

The name for Clifton's Cafeteria came from that of its founder, Clifford Clinton. His grandparents had come to San Francisco from Missouri in 1888 and entered the hotel and restaurant trade. By the early twentieth century the family operated a successful chain of cafeterias in San Francisco. Grandson Clifford left the enterprise in 1931 to open his own downtown eating place in Los Angeles, leasing the building on Olive Street. He and wife, Nelda, achieved their business goals, earning enough money to travel during the 1930s to the South Pacific and Asia, where they enjoyed collecting art, antiques, and décor. The couple then used these exotic souvenirs to help convert their downtown cafeteria into the Clifton's Pacific Seas Cafeteria in 1939.

Clifford and Nelda Clifton did not just cover the front of the eating place with tropical foliage and a waterfall. They did similar things inside, constructing a grotto-like stone entry and decorating the dining rooms with a reconstructed Polynesian thatch house, palm trees and giant flowers artistically crafted from neon electric tubes, and a "rain hut" on the mezzanine "where it rains every twenty minutes." Meals of typical American fare were accompanied by live organ music and performances by local singers on an "Aloha stage." In a side room near the entry, visitors walked into a re-creation of the Garden of Gethsemane in Jerusalem. There they might pray while viewing a kneeling figure of Christ sculpted by artist Marshall Lakey in 1943.

Clifton's Pacific Seas became a destination restaurant for both visitors and locals. It was only four blocks southeast of the original alignment of U.S. Highway 66 through downtown Los Angeles along South Figueroa Street. It became a favorite haunt for science fiction writer Ray Bradbury, and in *On the Road* Jack Kerouac described the Pacific Seas as "a cafeteria downtown which was decorated to look like a grotto." The remarkable themed restaurant operated until its closure in 1960.

R. E. York of Los Angeles, California, ordered 12,500 color postcards showing the façade of Clifton's Pacific Seas Cafeteria based on this tinted photograph. After receiving the materials on June 18, 1946, artists at the printing house enhanced the colors to create the postcard with stock number D-8253.

Aloha- Clifton's "Pacific Seas"
618 So. Olive St., Los Angeles

104

Aloha Stage, Clifton's Pacific Seas Cafeteria

1946

Los Angelinos knew Clifton's Pacific Seas Cafeteria as more than a place with exotic South Seas décor. They held operators Clifford and Nelda Clinton in high esteem for their generosity to the poor. The sign on the front of their cafeteria at 618 South Olive Street read, "Eat What You Wish," and this was just what they meant.

Clifford Clinton's father took his family, including the children, to China when he answered a call to missionary work there. The poverty and hunger the young Clifford saw in China left a deep impression on him, and the experience shaped the rest of his life. When he opened his cafeteria in 1931, the restaurateur set the policy that the enterprise would turn away no customers for lack of money. Any person who came to Clifton's hungry, even if penniless, received food. Typically the employees gave indigent diners the five-cent "Multi-Purpose Meal," which came in its own waxed cardboard container. According to the management, this concentrated repast contained "complete body nourishment for a third of the day." After 3:00 P.M. all customers received Clifton's own limeade beverage at no cost.

Nelda and Clifford Clinton went even further in their policies. Claiming that they made only half a cent in profit from each average forty-cent meal they served, the couple advertised widely that customers only had to pay what they thought their meals were worth. The bills patrons received stated plainly, "Regardless of amount of this check—our cashier will cheerfully accept whatever you wish to pay—or you may dine free." An information sheet the eatery distributed in the 1930s elaborated, "Our cashiers will not act snippy—and will graciously and unquestionably receive what you feel you wish to pay." In Charles Bukowski's 1982 novel *Ham on Rye*, a character remarked about Clifton's, "If you didn't have much money, they let you pay what you could."

In the summer of 1946, R. E. York of Los Angeles, California, ordered 12,500 color postcards based on this hand-colored print. Technicians at Curt Teich and Company received the materials by June 18, 1946, when they assigned the job stock number D-8254 and began production by augmenting the colors.

Aloha— Clifton's "Pacific Seas"
618 So. Olive St., Los Angeles

105

Waiting Room, Union Station

LOS ANGELES, CALIFORNIA

1939

The 1939 Los Angeles Union Station was the last monumental railway passenger terminal constructed in a major American city. Designed by architects John Parkinson and Donald B. Parkinson, it harmoniously combines Spanish Colonial Revival and Art Deco styles. The structure, which brought into one station the significant rail passenger lines serving the city, was built near the eighteenth-century Spanish Colonial heart of what had grown to become metropolitan Los Angeles. U.S. Highway 66 passed about eight blocks to the northwest, initially along Figueroa Street and then along the Arroyo Seco Parkway.

Voters approved construction of Union Station in 1926, but erection of the structure did not actually begin until 1934. Much of the original Los Angeles Chinatown occupied the site, so the project entailed considerable demolition. Work was finally completed on May 7, 1939. The busiest years for the terminal came during World War II, when an estimated one hundred trains came and went daily from Union Station tracks. Since that time rail passenger traffic has dwindled in volume, but at the time of writing the terminal continued to serve both Amtrak long-distance and Metrolink commuter trains.

The passenger waiting hall in the picture shows the building's blend of Spanish Colonial Revival and Art Deco styles. A steel gable structure that simulates wooden beams supports an exterior roof of mission-style red tiles. Cream-colored stucco covers the outside of the masonry walls, while the interior has marble and decorative hand-painted tiles, with a type of acoustical tile in upper areas. Red ceramic tile and swaths of geometrically shaped marble pieces in multiple colors cover the floors, simulating huge carpets. The open space measures 150 feet by 90 feet, with a 40-foot ceiling. Travelers still use the original large brown leather armchairs and benches.

The Western Publishing and Novelty Company, a postcard distributor in Los Angeles, placed an order for twenty-five thousand color postcards based on this retouched black-and-white photograph. The request made its way to Curt Teich and Company in Chicago by May 19, 1939, just days after the dedication of the terminal. Employees assigned the printing job stock number 9A-H918 and initiated production.

LA-29—Waiting Room, Union Station, Los Angeles, California

9A-H918

Earl Carroll Theatre-Restaurant

HOLLYWOOD, CALIFORNIA

1941

Broadway showman Earl Carroll went bust in New York after opening a lavishly overexpanded theater just as the Great Depression began, so he moved to California to try the same thing in Hollywood. The idea worked on the West Coast, and the 1938 Earl Carroll dinner theater at 6230 Sunset Boulevard was a smashing success. Here guests enjoyed extravagant meals accompanied by musical and comedy entertainment that included sixty dancing showgirls. Carroll decorated the front of his "entertainment palace" with a twenty-foot neon head of one of his entertainers, Beryl Wallace, and boldly declared to potential ticket buyers, "Through these portals pass the most beautiful girls in the world." U.S. Highway 66 motorists had easy access to Carroll's place of business, which lay only half a mile north of their east–west route along Santa Monica Boulevard.

Inside the seats and tables were on terraces, so all customers had unobstructed views of an enormous stage with a sixty-foot double revolving turntable and a staircase. The facility featured 6,200 feet of gold and blue neon lighting. World War II–era advertising invited customers to "dance to two famous orchestras, watch a CBS broadcast, and dine on superb dishes created by world-renowned chefs," adding, "The cost is remarkably little. $3.30 includes your deluxe dinner or only $1.65 without dinner." The ad specified that "evening clothes are not required" and that ladies "may come unescorted."

The high times came to an end with the death of Earl Carroll and Beryl Wallace in a 1948 airplane crash. The dinner theater soon thereafter became the Moulin Rouge, featuring Las Vegas–type acts; then the Hullabaloo rock-and-roll club; and then, in the 1960s, the Aquarius Theater for musical shows. The Pick-Vanoff Company purchased the old auditorium and converted it to a television production studio; actor Jerry Lewis used it for years as the setting for his Muscular Dystrophy Association charity telethons. In the 1990s the Nickelodeon cable television channel acquired the facility for production use, giving the building its current name, the Nickelodeon on Sunset.

The Western Publishing and Novelty Company placed an order for twenty-five thousand color postcards based on this retouched photograph. The request reached Curt Teich and Company in Chicago by October 29, 1941, when it received stock number 1B-H2155 and employees began preparing it for printing.

801—Earl Carroll Theatre-Restaurant, Hollywood, California

1B-H2155

239

Beverly Hills Hotel and Bungalows

BEVERLY HILLS, CALIFORNIA

1943

U.S. Highway 66 was a route for everyone, from those who stayed at the nicest lodgings to those who slept on the ground beside their cars. The Beverly Hills Hotel catered to the former class of travelers, and it predated the Mother Road by fourteen years. Drivers on Route 66 along North Santa Monica Boulevard easily accessed the big hotel by turning northwest at Beverly Gardens Park and proceeding a mile to the northwest along North Beverly Drive.

Built in the Mediterranean Revival style, the Beverly Hills Hotel opened to the public on May 12, 1912. It played a key role in a land promotion scheme to convert an attractive agricultural area west of Hollywood into a high-value residential development. Highway travel writer Thomas D. Murphy in 1915 called the lodging an "immense hotel" and described recently organized Beverly Hills as "a new resort town where many Los Angeles citizens have summer residences." Soon the rich and famous made Beverly Hills their own by building homes there.

The Beverly Hills Hotel, which offered guests twenty-three separate bungalows as well, became one of the premiere accommodations in California. Not only did people passing through Los Angeles stay there, but locals also used it as a gathering place for meetings out of the public eye. Tycoon Howard Hughes lived there off and on for thirty years, and famous guests included the Duke and Duchess of Windsor, Henry Fonda, and John Wayne. The inn was always exclusive. When preparing his 1949 guide to roadside lodging in America, travel writer Duncan Hines described the Beverly Hills Hotel as offering "every convenience for the comfort of guests," including multiple dining rooms, shops, a heated swimming pool, and lounges. He characterized it as "well managed and a pleasant place for overnight or longer" and added, "As in all extra good hotels, the rates are not cheap." It remained in commercial operation at the time of writing.

The Beverly Hills Hotel and Bungalows ordered twenty-five thousand color postcards based on this black-and-white photograph. It also enclosed a Kodachrome color photographic print as a guide for the artists creating the color postcard, noting, "Customer prefers soft subdued coloring." The materials reached the hands of Curt Teich and Company by August 3, 1943, when employees in Chicago created production file 3B-H983 and started production.

Beverly Hills Hotel and Bungalows
Beverly Hills, California

The Miramar

SANTA MONICA, CALIFORNIA

1935

Tracings its beginnings to the early days of Santa Monica, the Miramar Hotel and Apartments stand at the top of the Palisades bluffs overlooking the Pacific Ocean, about two blocks northwest of the traditional end of U.S. Highway 66.

John Percival Jones in 1872 joined with Robert S. Baker to purchase a former rancho along the Pacific coast and then laid out on its site an oceanfront town they named Santa Monica. They intended to sell lots in the town after reserving prime residential locations for themselves. Mining magnate Jones was serving as a U.S. senator from Nevada in 1888 when he constructed an impressive shingle-style home atop the bluffs facing the Pacific. He called the house Miramar, taking the name from the Spanish words *mira*, "view," and *mar*, "sea." Landscaping the grounds with native and exotic plants, he resided there until his death in 1912. Next the mansion went into the hands of King Gillette, the inventor of Gillette razor blades, and then it passed to hotelier J. C. H. Ivins.

About 1921 Los Angeles investor Gilbert F. Stevenson purchased the large city block including the residence, and in 1924 he erected at its northwest end an L-shaped reinforced-concrete hotel/apartment building in the Renaissance Revival style. Guests and residents could walk across the manicured grounds, cross Ocean Avenue, and descend to the Miramar Beach Club on the water for swimming and other seaside activities. In later years a substantial single-story administration building was connected to the 1924 building, the Jones mansion was removed, and bungalows and a swimming pool were added. Finally, in 1959 a multistory Ocean Tower was built. At the time of writing, the facility remained popular among Santa Monica visitors as the Fairmont Miramar Hotel and Bungalows.

The Miramar Hotel placed a request for 12,500 color postcards based on this black-and-white aerial photograph showing the complex in the mid-1930s. The order reached Curt Teich and Company by April 25, 1935, when it was assigned stock number 5A-H831.

5⅛

THE MIRAMAR — SANTA MONICA, CALIFORNIA

5A-H831

Belle-Vue French Café

SANTA MONICA, CALIFORNIA

1941

Established in 1937, the Belle-Vue French Café was for decades one of the popular restaurants offering continental fare in metropolitan Los Angeles. Its doors opened onto the traditional end of U.S. Highway 66, the intersection of Santa Monica Boulevard with Ocean Avenue on the seafront in Santa Monica.

Though it occupied a premier location, the Belle-Vue began as a modest local eatery. Proprietor James Wallace built it into a culinary destination specializing in fresh fish but also featuring beef, pork, and chicken dishes. A former chef, Eddie Pilloni, and his wife, Stella, purchased the restaurant in 1963, and in 1967 they brought in French-born chef Robert Lalli to take charge of the kitchen. Following Pilloni's death in 1976, his son Louis and daughter Denise Banks assumed management; Lalli stayed on as the creative force.

Lalli made his bouillabaisse a legend among the Belle-Vue's regulars. The hearty soup, served with a bib and only on Fridays, consisted of lobster, white fish, clams, scallops, and shrimp in a broth flavored with onions and saffron. It was delicious. One customer during the late 1960s claimed to have consumed 250 bowls and said he was looking forward to returning to the bistro on upcoming Fridays to have more.

In time the Belle-Vue came to be seen by ever-restless Los Angelinos as passé. Other French restaurants had opened in Santa Monica, and one of them even flew its chefs back and forth to kitchens in France. Diners began to see such Belle-Vue standards as sautéed rabbit in mustard cream sauce as "pleasant in its plush, antique way," but old-fashioned and overly rich. The customer base, mostly retirees, was not enough to keep the restaurant open. The old-time Route 66 eating place closed in 1991. The Crocodile Café occupied the building for a while, followed in 2004 by the BOA Steakhouse, but neither of these good restaurants could offer anything like the ambience of the old-time Belle-Vue.

In summer 1941, the Belle-Vue French Café sent Curt Teich and Company an order for sixty-five hundred color postcards based on this black-and-white photograph. The materials reached Chicago by August 4, 1941, the day Teich personnel gave the job stock number 1B-H1368 and started the printing process.

BELLE-VUE FRENCH CAFE — SANTA MONICA, CALIFORNIA

Club del Mar

1950

From the late nineteenth century onward, Santa Monica was the favorite location of Los Angelinos seeking seaside entertainments. Its oceanfront was punctuated with bathhouses, hotels, ballrooms, and amusement piers. The popular waterfront area boomed during the prosperous 1920s, but not every bather wanted to rub shoulders with working-class holidaymakers who flooded in from the city. Many well-off bathers wanted to enjoy the water and the cool sea breezes, but without the masses. This desire for exclusivity led to the creation of a dozen private beach clubs along the shore.

The 1922 Santa Monica Athletic Club led the way as the first private beach club at Santa Monica, but the Club del Mar and others quickly followed. Designed by Los Angeles architect Charles F. Plummer and built in 1924, the U-shaped, five-story, masonry Club del Mar faced the beach. Construction of the Mediterranean Renaissance Revival–style building was estimated to have cost $750,000, but the investment was worthwhile. The Club del Mar operated profitably as the largest of all the private beach clubs at Santa Monica, with a membership of almost two thousand. It counted among its members film actress Theda Bara and composer Rudolph Friml. Motorists on U.S. Highway 66 could reach it easily, since the club was located at 1910 Ocean Front Walk, only about five blocks southeast of the juncture of Santa Monica Boulevard and Ocean Avenue—the traditional end of the Mother Road.

The Club del Mar functioned solely as a private beach club into the 1930s, when it added hotel services. During World War II it provided temporary lodging and recreation for armed services members, and afterward it continued operating as a hotel and beach club into the 1950s. The facility became headquarters for the Synanon drug treatment program in 1959, then housed a Pritkin Longevity Center from 1978 to 1997. Owners of a nearby hotel acquired the Club del Mar in 1997, renovated the facility fully, and reopened it as a luxury hotel in 1999.

The Club del Mar placed an order for six thousand black-and-white postcards based on this photograph of the hotel as seen from the beach. The materials reached Curt Teich and Company at Chicago by November 1, 1950, when staff members assigned it stock number D-9704.

5 9/16 Square

Beach at Club del Mar

1950

The natural beach at Santa Monica was narrow and subject to erosion from storms. Consequently several breakwaters were built offshore in 1920 to augment the deposit of sand along the shore areas. This effort resulted in the creation of the broad expanses of sand that visitors see and enjoy today.

The enhanced beaches of Santa Monica became the setting for the creation of the modern sport of beach volleyball, which has been an Olympic competition event since 1996. Although the first known recorded beach volleyball was played in Hawaii about 1915, the game was perfected on the beaches at Santa Monica. Most of the early teams consisted of six players on each side. In 1930, however, Paul "Pablo" Johnson, while waiting for other players to arrive for a game at Santa Monica, proposed playing with fewer contestants on each side. This improvisation gave rise to the modern competition game. Although it continues to be played recreationally with more people, the most widely performed version pits two players on each side against each other. In all of the elite competition today, including Olympic-level games, each team has two participants.

The photograph, made from an upper window of the Club del Mar, shows nets and posts for beach volleyball just beyond the sunbathing and children's play areas. The teams from this club, many of them college students, figured prominently in the evolution of the sport. As the quality of the play improved, the various beach clubs sponsored their own tournaments. The 1924 interclub matches were the first beach volleyball tournaments recorded in California.

The Club del Mar placed an order for six thousand black-and-white postcards based on this photograph. The paperwork and photo reached Curt Teich and Company in Chicago by October 31, 1950, the day staff members gave the job stock number D-9703 and began the printing process.

112

O. J. Bennett's Sea Food Grotto

1941

Many tourists drove the length of Route 66 and went all the way to the Pacific Ocean at Santa Monica. Local boosters, who "claimed" Will Rogers because he had a home in nearby Pacific Palisades, placed a bronze plaque at the intersection of Santa Monica Boulevard with Ocean Avenue (an unofficial ending point for Highway 66) designating it the Will Rogers Highway. Among the destinations for vacationers in Santa Monica was the nearby pleasure pier, and here Orie Judson Bennett served them superlative meals of fresh fish.

Iowa-born "Captain" Bennett opened his Sea Food Grotto on the north side of the Santa Monica Municipal Pier in April 1931. He placed it on the first T-extension on the north side, which gave his customers views of the beach, the ocean, and the Santa Monica Mountains. This position provided natural cross-ventilation from sea breezes, enhancing the eatery's appeal in the days before air-conditioning. Locals also knew the Sea Food Grotto as an "open-air casino" where they could enjoy bridge parties and low-profile gaming at the seashore.

Meals of fresh fish were the real attraction at Bennett's Sea Food Grotto, which was known widely for its seafood cocktails, clam chowder, and fish dinners; they were said to be as good as any served in renowned restaurants in San Francisco, New Orleans, and Baltimore. Food critic Duncan Hines visited the Grotto in 1947 and asked the proprietor for "something different in seafood." After dining on broiled barracuda, Hines declared that it was prepared "as I have never eaten fish before." The food authority was so impressed that from 1945 to 1957 he put Bennett's personal recipe for fried fish in his annual compilation of recipes from "Duncan Hines Approved" restaurants.

O. J. Bennett himself operated the Sea Food Grotto until his death in 1955. It continued serving fish dinners after his death, but in 1966 it was sold and became the Boathouse Restaurant. At the time of writing, the site of Bennett's Sea Food Grotto on Santa Monica Pier was occupied by the popular Bubba Gump Shrimp Company Restaurant.

During the summer of 1941, O. J. Bennett ordered sixty-five hundred composite color postcards based on these photographs. The packet of materials reached Curt Teich and Company on July 3, 1941, when employees there gave it stock number 1B-H1209.

"CALIFORNIA'S UNIQUE EATING PLACE"

BENNETT'S SEA FOOD GROTTO — SANTA MONICA PIER — SANTA MONICA, CALIFORNIA

INDEX

Emmenegger Nature Park (St. Louis, Mo.), 42

Environmental Protection Agency, 44

Erdmann, Elizabeth, 86

Erdmann, Leonard, 86

Escalante Hotel (Ash Fork, Ariz.), 179

Eureka, Mo., Bridge Head Inn near, 44–45

Fairmont Miramar Hotel and Bungalows (Santa
    Monica, Calif.), 242

Falk, Samuel, 114

Federal Writers' Project guidebook to Kansas, 74

Ferguson, Katherine Krause, 190

filling stations: Amboy, Calif., 214–15, 220; Bender's
    One Stop Super Service Station (Amboy,
    Calif.), 214–15; Boots Court (Carthage, Mo.),
    62; City Café and Texaco Station (Kingman,
    Ariz.), 202, 204–205; Ed Wright Tire Company
    (Tulsa, Okla.), 92–93; Kerby's Auto Camp
    (Seligman, Ariz.), 192–93; Lampe-Birkenback
    Garage (Springfield, Mo.), 58–59; Leland's Gulf
    (Tucumcari, N.M.), 144; in Ludlow, Calif., 216;
    Oldham's State Line Station (near Shamrock,
    Tex.), 118–19; operated by F. Homer Rice,
    128; Osterman Service Station (Peach Springs,
    Ariz.), 179, 194, 196, 200; Peach Springs
    Trading Post (Peach Springs, Ariz.), 198–99;
    Phillips Petroleum Company, 114; Pontiac Café
    and Service Station (Pontiac, Ill.), 12, 28–29;
    Pueblo Court Station (Amarillo, Tex.), 124–25;
    Rest Haven Motor Court (Springfield, Mo.),
    54–55; Roy's Free Camp Ground and Service
    Station (Kingman, Ariz.), 202–203; Texaco,
    118–19, 144, 204–205; in Tijeras Canyon, N.M.,
    162–63; Tower Station (Shamrock, Tex.), 120; in
    Tucumcari, N.M., 144–45; in Victorville, Calif.,
    222

fire, damage to buildings, 26, 32, 38, 212

Five & Dime General Store (Santa Fe, N.M.), 158

Flamingo Motel (Amarillo, Tex.), 124

Ford, John, 146, 206

Ford automobile dealership, 218–19

Fort Leonard Wood, Mo., 48

Fort Reno, Okla., 114

Francois French Restaurant (Pasadena, Calif.),
    228–29

Francois Giacomone Restaurant (Pasadena, Calif.),
    228

Fray Marcos Hotel (Williams, Ariz.), 179

Fred Harvey Company: egalitarianism in restaurants
    operated by, 176; El Garces Hotel, 210, 212–13;
    El Navajo Hotel, 174–77; Havasu Hotel, 190–91;

Indian arts marketed by, 154–55, 164; Indian
    Detours (sightseeing tours), 154, 156, 164, 174,
    180; La Fonda Hotel, 150–57; La Posada Hotel,
    178, 179, 180–85; postcards distributed by, 152–
    53, 164–65, 174–77, 180–97, 190–91; restaurant
    in Peach Springs, Ariz., 194

Front Street (Needles, Calif.), 210–11

Funk's Grove, Ill., 13

F. W. Woolworth stores, 60, 158–59, 224–25

Galena, Kans., 80; Main Street in, 74–75; Tourist
    Camp in, 76–77; Travelers' Inn in, 78–79

Galley West Restaurant (Times Beach, Mo.), 44

Gallup, N.M.: cultural center in, 174; El Navajo
    Hotel in, 156, 174–77

gambling, 250

Garcés, Francisco, 212

Garland, Judy, 190

Garland's Drive-In Restaurant (Oklahoma City,
    Okla.), 98–99, 100

Garrison, John R., 70

Gasconade River, Mo., 50–51

gasoline stations. See filling stations

Geary, Fred, 174–75

Germany: foods eaten in, 16; immigrants from, 7, 16

Giacomone, Francois, 228. See also Francois French
    Restaurant

Gillette, King, 242

Gillett-Oglesby Building (Lincoln, Ill.), 32

"giraffe houses" (stone veneer buildings), 35, 48–49,
    54–57, 86–87

glass blocks, 56

Glenrio, Tex./N.M., 117

Glorieta Pass, N.M., 141, 148

Golden Dragon Restaurant (Tucumcari, N.M.), 144

Grand Canyon, Ariz., 154, 179, 188

Grants, N.M.: Fourth of July parade in, 172–73;
    Route 66 in, 141; Yucca Hotel in, 172–73

Grapes of Wrath (motion picture). See under motion
    pictures

Great Depression, 32, 42, 46, 132, 158; ballroom
    dancing as a diversion during, 70; beginning of,
    28, 90; Civilian Conservation Corps during, 188;
    Earl Carroll Theatre-Restaurant opened during,
    238; effects of, on Greyhound Corporation, 20;
    effects of, on Hotel Louis Joliet, 22; La Posada
    Hotel construction coincides with, 182; oil
    production in Oklahoma during, 85, 108, 110;
    Works Progress Administration during, 54

Great Plains, crossed by Route 66, 3–4, 117

greenhouses, 136–37

National Studio (Oklahoma City, Okla.), 106

Needles, Calif., 209, 216, 218; El Garces Hotel in, 210, 212–13; Front Street in, 210–11; transportation hub at, 210

Neely, Pleas, 62

neon ornamentation: at Clifton's Pacific Seas Cafeteria, 232–33, 235; at Earl Carroll Theatre-Restaurant, 238–39

neon signage: at Boots Court, 62–63; at El Fenix Restaurant, 100–101; at Herman's Restaurant, 110; at Longchamp Dining Salon, 128–29; at Morton's Restaurant, 20; at Phillips Courts, 114–15; at Rest Haven Motor Court, 54; at Sooner State Motor Kourt, 86–87; at Sylvan Beach Restaurant, 42

New Mexico, 4, 10–11, 140–77; state flower of, 85

New Yorker Hotel Orchestra, 108–109

Nichols Drug Store (Baxter Springs, Kans.), 80, 82

Nickel, George, 120

Nickelodeon on Sunset (Hollywood, Calif.), 238

nightclubs, 64; Aquarius Theater, 238; Earl Carroll Theatre-Restaurant, 209, 238–39; Holiday Inn Ballroom, 70–71; Hullabaloo rock-and-roll club, 238; Moulin Rouge, 238; Old Tascosa Room, 132–33; Venetian Room, 108–109. *See also* cocktail lounges

Oasis Café (Ludlow, Calif.), 208, 220

Oasis Café (Victorville, Calif.), 222–23

Oasis Hotel (Ludlow, Calif.), 218–19

Oatman, Ariz., 179

O'Connor, John L., 38

O. C. Osterman Auto Court (Peach Springs, Ariz.), 200–201

O'Havre, William, 48

O. J. Bennett's Sea Food Grotto (Santa Monica, Calif.), 209, 250–51

Oklahoma, 3, 11, 84–115; legislature, 94, 112

Oklahoma City, Okla., 3; automobile sales and service in, 102–103; Beverly's Chicken in the Rough Restaurants in, 94–97; El Charrito Restaurant in, 100, 104; El Charro Restaurant in, 104–105; El Fenix Restaurant in, 100–101; emergency medical services authority in, 104; Garland's Drive-In Restaurant in, 98–99; Herman's Restaurant in, 110–11; McDonald-Scott Chevrolet Company in, 102–103; Patrick's Drive-In Food in, 112–13; Route 66 in, 85; Skirvin Hotel in, 84, 106–109

Oklahoma City Oil Field, 108, 110; derrick removed from photograph of, 96–97

Oklahoma State Capitol: proximity of, to Chicken in the Rough restaurant, 94; proximity of, to Garland's Drive-In Restaurant, 98; on Route 66, 85

Oldest Well in U.S.A. (Glorieta, N.M.), 148–49

Oldham's State Line Station (east of Shamrock, Tex.), 118–19

Old Riverton Store (Riverton, Kans.), 73

Old Tascosa Room (Amarillo, Tex.), 132–33

O'Malley, John, 24–25

O'Malley and Stitzer Drugstore (Dwight, Ill.), 13, 24–25

"On the Atchison, Topeka and Santa Fe" (song), 190

Osborne, Beverly, 85, 94–97

Osborne, Rubye, 85, 94–97

Osterman, John, 179, 194, 196, 200

Osterman, Oscar C., 179, 194, 196, 200

Ozark Mountains, Mo., 3, 35, 46, 48, 50, 68

Ozark stone buildings, 35, 48–49, 54–57, 86–87

Painted Desert, Ariz., 156, 179, 180

parades: in Grants, N.M., 72–73; in Pasadena, Calif., 228

Parkhurst, T. H., 150

parking garages, 58–59

Parkinson, Donald B., 236

Parkinson, John, 236

parks: Arroyo Seco Parkway (Los Angeles, Calif.), 230–31; Carter Park (Carthage, Mo.), 60–61; Emmenegger Nature Park (St. Louis, Mo.), 42; greenspace in St. Louis, 38; Junge Park (Joplin, Mo.), 66–67; Route 66 State Park (Eureka, Mo.), 42, 44; Santa Fe Park (Needles, Calif.), 210–11; Sylvan Beach Park (St. Louis, Mo.), 25, 42–43; Tourist Park (Carthage, Mo.), 60–61

Pasadena, Calif., 209; Arroyo Seco Parkway in, 230–31; Francois French Restaurant in, 228–29; landscape near, 228

Pasadena Freeway, Calif., 230

Patrick's Drive-In Food (Oklahoma City), 112–13

Peach Springs, Ariz.: birds-eye view of, 194–95; O. C. Osterman Auto Court in, 200–201; Peach Springs Auto Court in, 200; Peach Springs Trading Post in, 198–99

Pecos National Monument, N.M., 148

Pecos River, N.M.: crossings at Santa Rosa, 146–47; crossed by Route 66, 141, 146–47

Pennant Hotel (Rolla, Mo.), 46–47

Penniman (towboat), 36

Pepys, Mark, 176, 204

Peters, Louis, 42